Black Speculative Feminisms

NEW SUNS:

RACE, GENDER, AND SEXUALITY IN THE

SPECULATIVE

Susana M. Morris and Kinitra D. Brooks, Series Editors

Black Speculative Feminisms

Memory and Liberated Futures in Black Women's Fiction

Cassandra L. Jones

THE OHIO STATE UNIVERSITY PRESS
COLUMBUS

Copyright © 2024 by The Ohio State University.
All rights reserved.

Library of Congress Cataloging-in-Publication Data
Names: Jones, Cassandra L., author.
Title: Black speculative feminisms : memory and liberated futures in Black women's fiction / Cassandra L. Jones.
Other titles: New suns: race, gender, and sexuality in the speculative.
Description: Columbus : The Ohio State University Press, [2024] | Series: New suns: race, gender, and sexuality in the speculative | Includes bibliographical references and index. | Summary: "Examines how authors such as Octavia E. Butler, Tananarive Due, and Nnedi Okorafor use the tropes of science fiction and fantasy to examine the decolonization of time as a liberatory action, the danger to social movements in the re-creation of oppression, and the emotional cost and labor of social justice work"—Provided by publisher.
Identifiers: LCCN 2024026036 | ISBN 9780814215401 (hardback) | ISBN 0814215408 (hardback) | ISBN 9780814283776 (ebook) | ISBN 0814283772 (ebook)
Subjects: LCSH: American fiction—African American authors—History and criticism. | African American feminists. | American fiction—Women authors—History and criticism. | Speculative fiction—Women authors—History and criticism.
Classification: LCC PS153.B53 J66 2024 | DDC 810.9/896073—dc23/eng/20240812
LC record available at https://lccn.loc.gov/2024026036

Other identifiers: ISBN 9780814259290 (paperback) | ISBN 0814259294 (paperback)

Cover image by Black Kirby
Cover design by Laurence J. Nozik
Text composition by Stuart Rodriguez
Type set in Palatino Linotype

CONTENTS

Acknowledgmentsvii

IntroductionBlack Speculative Feminisms and Restorative Fabulation1

Chapter 1Memory as Horror and Healing in Tananarive Due's *The Good House* and Nalo Hopkinson's *The New Moon's Arms*13

Chapter 2Memory, Decolonization, and Alien Invasion in Nnedi Okorafor's *Lagoon*35

Chapter 3Memory and Time Travel in Octavia E. Butler's *Kindred* and Rasheedah Phillips's *Telescoping Effect: Part One*52

Chapter 4Memory and the Reproduction of Regime: Anyanwu as *Lieu de Mémoire* in Octavia E. Butler's Patternist Series69

ConclusionNext Steps as We Realize the World Is on Fire89

Bibliography95

Index103

ACKNOWLEDGMENTS

I would like to acknowledge the support—financial, physical, and emotional—of all the persons and entities that helped me complete this project. With the help of the Taft Research Center Fellowship at the Charles Phelps Taft Research Center at the University of Cincinnati, I was able to maintain a writing network even during quarantine. I would like to specifically thank Taft Center Director Amy Lind and Program Director Sean Keating for their guidance and support. In addition to the Center Fellowship, the Taft Research Center also generously provided support for research trips to the Huntington Library and various conferences to present pieces of the project.

I would like to thank my department, Africana Studies, at the University of Cincinnati for providing mentorship in navigating the various hurdles of university life. Joseph Takougang's institutional knowledge and commitment to relaxed service requests for junior faculty provided a much-needed support around saying no. Thanks to Holly Y. McGee, Sherae Daniel, Tia Gaynor, Brandi Blesset, Sharrell Luckett, Carolette Norwood, and the Black Faculty Association for your support and encouragement. Thanks so much for our weekly writing dates, for your patience in listening to my frustrations at developing ideas, and for providing emotional outlets, mentorship, and access to funds to support the development of the project.

In addition to the support I received from the University of Cincinnati, I would like to thank the University of South Carolina and USC Upstate, where I began this project. The Aspire Award from the Office of Research at the University of South Carolina subsidized my first two visits to the Huntington Library and my first weeks parsing the massive collection of Octavia E. Butler's papers. That first trip connected me with Ayana Jamieson and the rest of the Octavia E. Butler Legacy Network, who changed the trajectory of my career and my thinking around what scholarship and scholarly communities could look like. I would like to thank the USC Upstate Office of Sponsored Awards and Research Support for the guidance and feedback I received via their many workshops.

The Department of English and African American Studies at USC Upstate deserves special recognition as well. It was at this institution that I met the powerhouse known as Warren Carson who introduced me to the College Language Association and supported my growth as a teacher, scholar, and administrator. His mentorship will forever serve as my model for mentoring those around me. Thanks to June Carter, Carmen Harris, and the other members of the Faculty of Color Association who were my support network as I navigated the tenure-track system for the first time. Thanks to Roger A. Sneed who answered a random email and with whom I've since spent many hours discussing Star Trek.

Thanks to Tisha Brooks, Manu Chandler, Helene Lee, and the National Center for Faculty Development and Diversity. Thanks for supporting me through the transition from one institution to another and for helping me get back on track and stay on track with my daily writing practice.

Many thanks and much love go out to the Octavia Butler Legacy Network and Ayana Jamieson, Therí A. Pickens, Moya Bailey, Sami Schalk, Shelley Streeby, and Aimee Bahng, who are all amazing scholars and activists. Thanks to Nisi Shawl for sharing her stories about her friendship with Octavia and clues to what the third Parable book might be about.

Thanks as well to Kelly L. Watson, Rachel Dean-Ruzicka, Christine Hoffman, Angie Fitzpatrick, Kishonna L. Gray, and Takiyah Nur Amin for their friendship and support of my work.

Thanks to Maisha Wester, who inspired me and continues to embody the phrase "Black Excellence." Thanks for Don McQuarie, Radhika Gajjala, and Ellen Berry for believing in me and supporting my early work.

Finally, thanks to my parents and family, who have supported my many absences and flights of fancy. Thanks to Patrick Thomas for reading my nearly completed manuscript and assuring me that it was, in fact, a book. And, of course, to the fuzziest of friends, Colin Jones, who took many naps and walks with me to think through the ideas in these pages. I will forever appreciate the focus you gave me those mornings sitting by my side as I wrote, my fuzzy boy. I hope I sent you off to the next world with the care and love you deserve.

Portions of chapter 4 originally appeared as "Memory and Resistance: Doro's Empire, Mary's Rebellion, and Anyanwu as *Lieu de Mémoire* in Octavia E. Butler's Mind of My Mind and *Wild Seed*," *Women's Studies*, vol. 47, no. 7, 2018, © Taylor & Francis, https://doi.org/10.1080/00497878.2018.1518618.

INTRODUCTION

Black Speculative Feminisms and Restorative Fabulation

Exploring social media in recent years, so much of the work that I see Black women doing centers on keeping records, bringing other women's work to light, and supporting other women's work through networks in ways that appear magical and effortless. Indeed, these seemingly effortless "glow ups" are what CaShawn Thompson calls attention to with her hashtag #BlackGirlMagic: "I say 'magic' because it's something that people don't always understand. Sometimes our accomplishments might seem to come out of thin air, because a lot of times, the only people supporting us are other black women" (qtd. in Thomas). Additional hashtags such as #CiteHerWork make clear both these hidden networks and the attempted sidelining of Black women's contributions to academia and also act as digital extensions of the Black feminist tradition of producing knowledge from the margins. The hashtags #BlackWomenAreTheFuture and #ListenToBlackWomen equally suggest that Black women's positions offer special insight not only into contemporary forms of injustice and struggle but also have a clear stake in imagining, presenting, and creating liberated futures. Each of these examples is a form of memory preservation. For instance, #CiteHerWork asks us to remember who first posited a concept such as misogynoir, a concept developed by Moya Bailey, whose origins were at risk of being obscured. These hashtags and the everyday conversations via social media of scholars and activists worked to disrupt this potential erasure. In addition to the process of digitally archiving achievements, this memory-work asks us to remember our power and recognize that the joy and energy of conversations in the everyday can and do shape the ideas that will change our world.

Alongside these digital interventions, Black feminists have issued explicit calls for attention to record-keeping as an ongoing antiracist intervention. Christina Sharpe notes the systems of Black redaction and annotation as knowledge production that are shaped by historical and current traumas that she calls "wake work." They highlight the ways we are pushed and pulled and must act and react in response to these currents of the wake of Black diasporic history. Christina Sharpe calls for "new modes of writing, new modes of making-sensible" (114), and the digital orthographies of these hashtags are examples of the type of wake work to which Sharpe calls attention. These forms of written protest reject the redaction of our inner lives as well as the social and political work that are rendered "invisible to the present and future, subtended by plantation logics, detached optics, and brutal architectures" (Sharpe 114).

These recent Black feminist calls for annotation and citation are reiterations of an ongoing mobilization toward both remembering and recognizing the contributions of Black women and all Black people. This book collects the interventions of Black women writers of speculative fiction into the patriarchal, capitalist, and racist urge to forget under the umbrella of what I am calling "Black speculative feminisms." Authors such as Octavia E. Butler, Tananarive Due, Nalo Hopkinson, Nnedi Okorafor, and Rasheedah Phillips serve not simply as examples of theoretical frameworks in action but themselves offer radical frameworks by which we are invited to annotate our past, present, and future.

Butler's record-keeping carries on the tradition of annotation in the form of lineage records noted in the family bible, diaries, and cookbooks created from the notecards of home cooks, each with their own histories within Black American women's cultures. Just as historians of Black women's history have excavated these sources to understand the worlds of Black women, expanding the work of historians beyond public and official records, so too have Afrofuturist scholars examined Black writing as speculative, expanding our notion of Black literature to include science fiction and fantasy.

Linking both these worlds, Octavia E. Butler provides an example of the wake work or memory-work carried on via Black women's tradition of knowledge production from the margins in her lifetime's worth of meticulous record-keeping and the bequeathing of her papers to the Huntington Library archives. This annotation is an act of both radical reproduction and a map of Butler's own knowledge production (Streeby 719). Butler's note-taking highlights record-keeping and calls attention to existing archives of Black-produced knowledge. This equally gestures toward a long Black history taking us from *nommo* (the power of the word) in African American oral tradition all the way through to contemporary hashtags.

I briefly sketch these examples to turn attention toward the memory-work found in the novels and short stories of Black women. The novel is a didactic device with the power to connect us to meaning, teach our shared Black mythology, create communities, and instill an Afrocentric worldview with the potential to address the ongoing trauma of living in an anti-Black world (Morrison, "Rootedness"). These literary "homespaces" operate as a safe place to be ourselves, as a position from which to theorize, as Kinitra D. Brooks argues: "In this space of self-revelation, black women creators are freed from the constraints of literary respectability politics in which they must always be concerned with larger goals of black feminist goals of being deemed writers of literature" (72). Black women's writing is a "fluid fiction" that operates between genres such as horror, science fiction, fantasy, and historical realism and emerges as a speculative act that rejects the genre definitions that are used to dismiss our contributions (Brooks 72). Toni Morrison equally notes the relegation of women's writing to genre writing such as "magical realism" as a means of dismissal: "For literary historians and literary critics [magical realism] just seemed to be a convenient way to skip again what was the truth in the art of certain writers" (qtd. in Davis 414). While Morrison argues that Black women's writing offers us insight into the issues facing us and need not serve as a "recipe" for solving those problems ("Rootedness" 58–59), Black women's speculative fiction, as visionary fiction, does offer, if not solutions outright, at least paradigm shifts that can offer new questions. These questions and potential solutions offer "new ways of making-sensible," and the fluidity of Black women's speculative fiction explores that uneasy amalgamation of "real" and fantastic, object and metaphor, and offers an unusual means of annotating those material histories where Black emotional and intellectual interiority are redacted.

Drawing from an exploration of lived experience as a crèche of theorization, a key tenet of Black feminist thought, this book examines speculative literature written by Black women as they express various forms of restorative fabulation, employing multiple forms of memory including individual and cultural or collective memory, commemoration, bodily memory and trauma that the body remembers, and rememory as avenues for imagining the world as a fairer and more just place, for reimagining the past, and as method of expressing emotion, even considering vengeance and catharsis.

Indeed, as Audre Lorde and Brittney Cooper both note, we must make room for unpleasant emotions like rage. To avoid complete collapse into the utopian impulse, as Morris, Hartman, Lorde, and Cooper each warn us in their separate ways, we suppress our three-dimensional humanity when we refuse to recognize the wide range of feelings.[1] Speculative fiction or "fluid fiction," the literary homespace for Black women that is genre-defying, slippery, existing between fact and interpretation, metaphor and object, in defiance of the respectability literary politics, is a cauldron for creation and of possibility, providing a ripe site of interrogation.

When I began to think about how Black women have explored this cultural work through speculative texts, I was first inspired by rereading Octavia E. Butler's *Mind of My Mind* and *Wild Seed* to examine Anyanwu's role as a source of neglected cultural memory and the untapped instructive power she carried. Although written well after the Patternist series, one of Butler's own stated goals in the Parable series is to instruct: "In '[*Parable of the Sower*],' I point out all the problems living the way we do has brought upon us. In its sequel '*Parable of the Talents*,' . . . I try to offer some solutions" (Octavia E. Butler Papers,[2] box 327, folder 1). The archives of Butler's work and personal notes reveal the ways in which the creation of each of her universes are intertwined and at times co-constitutive.

The study of Octavia E. Butler brought me to the OEB Legacy Network and observation of the emergence of Black speculative feminisms from scholar/activists such as adrienne maree brown, Walidah Imarisha, Moya Bailey, Therí Pickens, Sami Schalk, Ayana Jamieson, Kinitra Brooks, Susana M. Morris, Kameelah L. Martin, and Alexis Pauline Gumbs. Their work is concerned with recovering histories, examining futurity and forward-looking chronopolitics, the physicality of the body and disability, traditional African religion, conjure, and alternative ways of knowing in and around literature as broader sources of inspiration for social change. These theorists equally define and operate from Afrofuturist feminism and/or Black ecofeminism, looking to slime molds, sea life, and nature's fractals to consider how we might more accurately recognize each other's humanity, socially organize in intentional and inclusive ways, disrupt our sense of Homo sapiens supremacy, and extend our sense of time beyond the anthropocene. In defining Black speculative feminisms, I build from the claim that all activist and feminist work is already, by its very nature, speculative in that it

---

1. I take inspiration as well from Natalie Diaz's notion of "alongsideness," where she argues that we must find ways to live with positions and people who are antithetical to our own.

2. Hereafter OEBP.

illuminates problems and participates in the ideation and construction of a world in which these social ills are cured. However, I employ the phrase "Black speculative feminisms" to participate in the ongoing recasting of Black speculative literature as a vector of Black feminist praxis, drawing Black women's speculative fiction more directly into conversations about Black feminist thought as contributors themselves rather than simply reflections of feminist discourse, to mark these authors as movement intellectuals who shape the aims and values of Black speculative feminisms. Indeed, Black feminist author/activists adrienne maree brown, Alexis Pauline Gumbs, and Rasheedah Phillips expressly cite the work of other Black women speculative authors as direct inspiration for their critical interventions.

"Afrofuturist feminism," a term coined by Susana M. Morris, is "a reflection of the shared central tenets of Afrofuturism and black feminist thought [that] reflects a literary tradition in which people of African descent and transgressive, feminist practices born of or from across the Afrodiaspora are key to a progressive future" ("Black Girls" 156). Moving beyond the literary, Morris notes the ways Afrofuturist feminists employ art, music, fashion, and cultural criticism to create an Afrocentric perspective, inheriting many lessons from the Black Arts Movement of the 1960s and 1970s. Offering an unapologetic and fully agentic Black womanhood through the lens of science fiction and fantasy tropes, these stories and social commentary are "key to progressive futures" ("Black Girls" 156). However, Morris is careful to note that these stories do not collapse into rigid feminist utopias, but remain malleable worlds inspired by feminist principles and ideas.

Although Morris does not foreclose the possibility of Black ecofeminism within her definition of Afrofuturist feminism, I use Black speculative feminisms to expand Morris's description to both include and highlight a growing interest in food justice, farming, and ecological concerns as chronopolitical[3] antiracist and antisexist work that intersects with Black and Indigenous storytelling and overlooked technological contributions. This aligns with Elizabeth A. Wheeler's discussion of "afroaquanauts" in both Afrofuturist literature and Black activist circles who equip themselves with protective technologies of survival to wade through anti-Black waters: "Afroaquanauts need life support systems to navigate hostile terrain: systems like clean water, access to health care and disability services, and an

---

3. Kodwo Eshun's notion of chronopolitics invites Black Studies scholars to look to questions of the future alongside our desire to reconstitute histories and excavate the issues of the present. Taking this view, he argues, allows us to intervene in the work of techno-futurists who have no investment in considering the role of race, racism, or anti-Blackness in their vision of what is to come.

end to state violence" (173). Drawing on the cognitive estrangement of Afrofuturism, Wheeler demonstrates how Black speculative fiction exposes both injustice such as environmental racism and the imagination necessary to address them (172). In addition to expanding toward environmental and food justice concerns, my intention is also to distance my larger argument from the antifeminist elements present within Afrofuturist circles who see Afrofuturism as an opportunity to recreate the most toxic elements of Black Power and Black Arts movements, such as excluding Black women and queer Black people, reaffirming limiting gender roles, and foregrounding Black men's claim to power within an unquestioned patriarchal order.

Under the larger umbrella of Black speculative feminisms, I define restorative fabulation as an aspect of Black critical imagination or the therapeutic act of imagining liberated Black futures. In this, I am inspired by Octavia E. Butler's own reflection: "My writing—my novels in particular—can be a kind of therapy for me and I'm sure some of their origins extend well back into my childhood" (OEBP, box 146, OEB 2927). I borrow "restorative" from the notion of restorative justice, a form of criminal justice that focuses not on the punitive but provides a frame that recognizes the damage incurred by acts of violence or theft and seeks to repair the social fabric of the community and reincorporate offenders into this social fabric rather than expel them to the margins of community through punitive action. Relationships and community, rather than property and punishment, are centered. I am drawn to this notion of restoration of community and the work of imagining and writing as forms of seeking justice, or as adrienne maree brown and Walidah Imarisha call it, "visionary fiction."

Restorative fabulation is inspired, of course, by critical fabulation, a writing and reading practice defined by Saidiya Hartman that highlights the limits of the practice of history of slavery and the colonial archive:

> The stories that exist are not about [these Black women and girls], but rather about the violence, excess, mendacity, and reason that seized hold of their lives, trans-formed them into commodities and corpses, and identified them with names tossed-off as insults and crass jokes. The archive is, in this case, a death sentence, a tomb, a display of the violated body, an inventory of property, a medical treatise on gonorrhea, a few lines about a whore's life, an asterisk in the grand narrative of history. (2)

Critical fabulation is not entirely an act of counter-memory that fills in the violated and erased voices in the archive, acknowledging the impossibility of the task of rewriting the past. Writing about a woman named Venus only noted briefly within historical archives, Hartman notes, "I feared what I might invent, and it would have been a romance" (8). Indeed, romanticizing the past is a criticism frequently leveled at scholars of African and African American history and literature. Certainly, as African Americans we have a tendency toward a romantic view of precolonial Africa and to imagine ourselves as dethroned kings and queens living in a "new world" that despises our existence. This popular narrative provides strength and acts as a balm to the anti-Black narratives that pervade American culture. Unfortunately, this utopian view neglects the complex realities of African life in the past as well as the present and serves to distance ourselves from these realities. This leads to a fear of not doing history "properly." But what I find powerful about Hartman's comment about her fear of imagining what those last moments of Venus's life might have been like was not this Black American utopian impulse to cast ourselves as previously powerful, wealthy inheritors, but rather humanizing a figure and imagining her huddled with her friend, holding her moments before that friend passed away. The imagined moments cannot change the past but help us understand how to live with the contradictions and attempted erasures of persons from it. This gesture, "situated between two zones of death—social and corporeal death" (Hartman 12), follows in the footsteps of the fictional retelling of Margaret Garner and other women in the neo-slave narratives written by Black women in the 1970s through the 1990s. Indeed, Hartman names Octavia E. Butler's *Kindred* as an example of this kind of imaginative thinking that cannot change the past but can breathe life into the historical record and shift our relationship with the past (14). "Narrative restraint, the refusal to fill in the gaps and provide closure, is a requirement of this method, as is the imperative to respect black noise—the shrieks, the moans, the non-sense, and the opacity, which are always in excess of legibility and of the law and which hint at and embody aspirations that are wildly utopian, derelict to capitalism, and antithetical to its attendant discourse of Man" (Hartman 12). Listening to the uneasy past as it calls from beyond the archive and resisting a desire to paper over it is key to this practice.

Joining the terms "restorative" and "fabulation" may remind the reader of therapeutic visualization exercises employed to imagine possible futures. This builds on and borrows from mindfulness strategies employed to quiet the mind as well as visualization used explicitly as a problem-solving tool. Because the acts of writing and oral storytelling require quiet reflection and purpose, particularly as life pulls us in all its many directions with unending distractions and traumas, it provides an opportunity to imagine different ways of operating in the world. Restorative fabulation recognizes the emotional labor of the author and serves as a balm for reckoning with those histories of trauma.

As Butler described her writing overall as therapeutic, so too did she note that writing *Kindred* was depressing. "I had to go places that I didn't enjoy going, in my own mind and in history. Also, my characters in *Kindred* couldn't really win. I couldn't change history and make them win" (Burton-Rose 202). In contrast, Butler described writing *Wild Seed,* in which characters equally grapple with chattel slavery, as a pleasurable process and as a "reward for having written *Kindred*" (Burton-Rose 202). In this way, Butler employs a process of restorative fabulation, using storytelling to create a world in which characters reckoning with chattel slavery are not yoked to realist history and provide both author and reader with an opportunity to shift our perspective and relationship to history, intensifying the existing agency of historical actors.

The work of imagining and writing are frequently invoked as tools of meaning-making and healing. Similar to Saidiya Hartman's conflicted relationship with the archives, Educator S. R. Tolliver's notion of "endarkened storywork" explores the relationship between remembering, listening, and storytelling in qualitative research as it conflicts with Eurocentric research methods. "In [*Recovering Black Storytelling in Qualitative Research*] and in this moment, I reclaim my history, excavating the storied ways of my ancestors to recover and remember what I've been taught to forget. Through this work, I make myself whole, stitching together parts of me that have been ruptured by the consistent need to place standard research documents above my desire to witness, to exhort, to sing praises, to tell stories" (Tolliver xvi). For Tolliver, writing is a source of reclamation, redemption, and unifying disparate parts of herself: the researcher trained in Eurocentric traditions and the Black woman whose interests in and experience with storytelling have brought her to academia. At once her book offers a strategy for allowing these two identities to work together for researchers such as herself and offers Tolliver herself an opportunity to reflect on the trauma of severing one's identity from one's training and to write herself a way to heal that trauma. This example reveals the twin axes of restorative fabulation: the ways in which storytelling can be a reclamation of identity, history, and/or memory and how it works simultaneously for the reader and the writer.

Of course, not all storytelling does progressive work. As we know, it is continually and disastrously present in the leaps made by journalists telling stories about young Black folks killed by police. Those storytellers of the nightly news are imagining the lives of those killed and imagining what their audience wants to know when they choose which images to display, mugshot or graduation photo. For this reason, I join "restorative" with "fabulation" to highlight the progressive and reparative form of imagining that I am invoking with the phrase. Restorative fabulation is critical as well as deliberately cognizant of the weight and impact of emotions on the writer and the community.

Since beginning this project in 2013, the literary world has exploded with the speculative fiction of Black women around the diaspora and from the continent. Novels by Nisi Shawl and Andrea Hairston have emerged to join their short stories, N. K. Jemison has created her fantastic worlds, and so many others such as Rivers Solomon, Justina Ireland, and Alaya Dawn Johnson have published work that would fit comfortably within this analysis of memory. Despite this, I have drawn boundaries to create a tightly focused project exploring a corpus of literary Afrofuturism and African Futurism specifically interrogating memory from Octavia E. Butler's novels in the 1970s through to Rasheedah Phillips publications from 2017, touching on authors and activists, like those mentioned above, who consider themselves among what Walidah Imarisha and adrienne maree brown refer to as "Octavia's Brood."

Drawing on a growing body of scholarship that analyzes haunting and the use of ghosts in horror fiction, chapter 1, "Memory as Horror and Healing in Tananarive Due's *The Good House* and Nalo Hopkinson's *The New Moon's Arms*," examines how Black women writing speculative fiction employ memory as a tool for familial and communal healing as well as identifying spiritual and existential threats to the community. Analyzing Tananarive Due's *The Good House* and Nalo Hopkinson's *The New Moon's Arms*, I argue that these authors position forgetting one's family or cultural legacy as a source of horror or tension in their stories, while reconnecting with the past represents the resolution of those tensions.

The Good House features a family matriarch who, in her youth, angered the gods in her hubris and, in shame at the harm she brings to her own daughter, attempts to hide the family's legacy from her grandchild and great-grandson. However, breaking the family lineage of knowledge and spiritual power threatens to not only end the Toussaint family, but destroy the entire community. Eschewing typical representations of Hoodoo and Vodou as horrific and stories of haunting where the trauma remembered or the trauma that cannot be forgotten is the locus of horror, Due provides a story where the act of forgetting is the trauma that must be repaired. In order to save the family line and the community at large, Marie, Angela, and Corey work across time and states of being to restore familial memory and spiritual legacy.

The New Moon's Arms equally features a family secret that has left Calamity estranged from her daughter and grandchild. When Calamity's father dies, the memories and family secrets about the disappearance of her mother come pouring forward, coinciding with Calamity's hot flashes and imminent menopause. Alongside these revelations, Calamity discovers a special child washed up on the shore who connects the world of her fictional Caribbean island home to the African ancestors brought to the area via the trans-Atlantic slave trade. Calamity's desire to make this child's body and behavior fit into existing cultural molds reflects her own traumatic upbringing and the generational trauma she has inflicted on those she loves most in her life. As Calamity discovers how she's been forced to interpret her own actions through sexist and racist colonial lenses, her memories of family are unlocked and she is able to repair current relationships.

The restorative fabulation of Hopkinson and Due offers a means to recognize the emotional impact of racist, sexist, and homophobic frameworks' limitations on our perceived possibilities and how these damaging frameworks shape our interpretations of ourselves, providing the fluid boundaries of "real" and "magical" as a space to define ourselves, our families, and our histories, reflecting Black speculative feminisms' continuing attention to the power of self-definition.

While chapter 1 centers on the compulsion to forget as a mechanism of oppression, chapter 2, "Memory, Decolonization, and Alien Invasion in Nnedi Okorafor's *Lagoon*," examines the power of restorative fabulation to fuse cultural memory and the perspective shift necessary to expunge the vestiges of colonial influence on African nations. The focus of this chapter is Nnedi Okorafor's *Lagoon*, a novel that imagines an alien invasion acting as a force for decolonization rather than the more frequent version of invasion in which humans unite in battle against an off-world force of destruction. Tales of invasion typically represent cultural anxiety about loss of control or fears that colonizers will, in turn, become colonized. Instead, Okorafor uses the trope as an opportunity to drastically reimagine relationships and power structures. *Lagoon* displaces human/animal binaries as well as gender and racial cultural hierarchies while drawing on specifically West African, Nigerian, and ethnic cultures and existing resistance movements. This chapter demonstrates how Black women's visionary fiction provides readers with a sense of the depth of change necessary for decolonization that supports the subsequent chapter's suggestion that the decolonization of time is a potential vector of radical change.

Chapter 3, "Memory and Time Travel in Octavia E. Butler's *Kindred* and Rasheedah Phillips's *Telescoping Effect: Part One*," approaches decolonization from the perspective of Western and non-Western notions of time, taking Octavia E. Butler's *Kindred* and Rasheedah Phillips's novella *Telescoping Effect: Part One* as its focus. While many scholars have examined *Kindred* as an example of the neo-slave narrative genre, this chapter places Butler's work in the emerging context of what John Jennings refers to as *sankofarration*, which looks at how Black authors seek to recover not just lost histories but also non-Western conceptions of time itself. John Mbiti described traditional African time as a two-dimensional model that constructs time in relationship to community ties. Composed of the Sasa, the recently deceased with people still alive who knew them, and the Zamani, the deceased with no living person left to remember them directly, this concept privileges the communal and how our understanding of history shifts over time. Rasheedah Phillips, as both author and activist, explores the Western colonization of concepts of temporality and, like Butler, how family lineage provides pathways for "going back for what was left behind." Drawing together the relationship between memory and an understanding of time as iterative, the authors' restorative fabulation provides the radical possibilities for social organization and emotional healing that emerge when we change our understanding of time.

Focusing on Octavia E. Butler's Patternist series, "Memory and the Reproduction of Regime: Anyanwu as *Lieu de Mémoire* in Octavia E. Butler's Patternist Series," chapter 4, explores how Black women's speculative fiction serves as a tool for imagining worlds beyond the legacy of colonization, while focusing on the dangers of recreating oppression when we choose not to remember the past as we build these futures. This chapter examines Anyanwu, the immortal shapeshifter from *Mind of My Mind* and *Wild Seed*, as *lieu de mémoire*, or as cultural and historical touchstone, and the failure to utilize lessons from the past at the dawn of Patternist society.

As the Patternists built their culture, they created a shared history complete with educational blocks imbued with collective memory. Collective memory is defined here as recollections of a shared past "that are retained by members of a group, large or small, that experienced it" (Schuman and Scott, 361–62). The use of collective memory as means to create a shared identity has a long lineage in Black American history. The memories shared by these groups are passed on through acts of public commemoration in which ceremonies, rituals, or other discourses are created to establish a shared past (Eyerman 65). As a story that provides a sense of the group's origins, their past and future, this collective memory of the Patternist was built without any connection to the historical struggles of Black people, Indigenous peoples, or People of Color, including racism, sexism, or homophobia.

In addition, by refusing to tap into Anyanwu as *lieu de mémoire*, the new radical structure that the community hoped would free them from economic and social struggle ultimately recreated the discrimination they faced with a new class of humans, mutes, serving as the societal scapegoat. This chapter demonstrates how Black women's speculative fiction reminds readers of the importance of memory in forward-looking agendas.

Taken together, these authors represent a contribution toward the development of Black speculative feminisms, or a community of scholars, activists, and artists who operate in a circular manner. Praxis seems to fail in its description of the activities of this community. While praxis suggests theory-informed activism—and certainly, some forms of responsive feminisms are shaped by the work of activists—frequently there is an assumption of unidirectional movement, from academia toward activism. While Black feminisms, as rooted in the lived experiences of women, are multidirectional and frequently move in the direction of activism toward academia with, for instance, branches of blues and hip-hop feminisms taking inspiration from music and bringing those conversations and shapes of genders, bodies, and movements into academia, Black speculative feminisms triangulate these flows, bringing together art, scholarship, and activism into conversation, each equally inspiring the other, adopting the most fruitful connections from previous movements such as the Black Power and Black Arts movements, while jettisoning those that are no longer useful. This work focuses on the memory-work of Black women's speculative fiction, but Black speculative feminisms equally explore music, fashion, fine and plastic arts, film, video games, or any work that challenges us to rethink our engagement with race, oppression, definitions of reality, history, the present, and the future, making specific room for Black ecofeminist reclamations of relationships with land and environment beyond the capitalist framework of extraction and efficiency. Within the larger framework of Black feminist thought, this work considers speculative fiction as an entry in Black women's annotative theory, where literature and the invitation to imagine possible futures and realities converge with Black women's memory-work. Doing so cements both Afrofuturism's call to recognize the intermingling of past, present, and future, and equally Kodwo Eshun's, Octavia E. Butler's, and adrienne maree brown's calls to shape a more just future by imagining Black people in it.

CHAPTER 1

Memory as Horror and Healing in Tananarive Due's *The Good House* and Nalo Hopkinson's *The New Moon's Arms*

White horror narratives often invite the audience to forget, particularly where Black history and trauma is concerned. As audience members, we know the protagonist should not open the door, enter the basement, go into the woods, or invoke a spirit in the mirror. Black audiences often speak back, imploring the characters on screen not to do this. The film *Skeleton Key* (2005) features a white woman who opens herself to possession and body theft by beginning to believe in Voodoo, a Hollywood version of the very real spiritual belief system known as Vodou. The 1991 version of *Candyman* centers on a white woman seeking to make her name in academia, who, while investigating the murder of a young Black woman in the Cabrini Green projects, calls Candyman's name in the mirror and denounces him to his community, opening herself and her loved ones up to his murderous revenge. Each of these films carry the message that to examine and believe the stories of Black people will lead to gruesome and terrifying death; to remember the trauma and tragedies of Black history is dangerous. Indeed, these underlying narratives of fear of Black history motivates the current political attacks on critical race theory in K–12 schools and universities across the United States. According to the rhetoric of the political right, learning these histories of violence and resistance not only threatens the mental well-being of the students learning them, but is dangerous to the very fabric of the country.

However, to remember does not always serve to haunt and horrify as white horror (and political) narratives suggest. Black film and literature are often venues for what Kameelah Martin terms "Black Feminist Voodoo Aesthetics." From African American folktales of the oral tradition where conjurors fought illness and disease and used their powers to soothe tensions in Black communities, to the stories of Charles Chestnutt who depicted conjure women as folk heroes who subverted the power of white slaveholders, these stories celebrate conjure as a site of spiritual and cultural power for Black women and as a repository for spiritual practices that bind us to an African past (Martin, *Envisioning*). These traditions are vital and are certainly not meant to be forgotten. Tananarive Due's *The Good House,* a speculative novel about the family of a conjure woman, situates the story's horror in the failure to remember. In Due's tale, to forget symbolically reenacts the same violence that was done under the yolk of slavery in which Black women were severed from familial connection. By using the mechanism of memory to resolve the narrative horror of the novel, Due's story represents how Black women's speculative literature employs remembrance to venerate and acknowledge the presence of the ancestral while also, in the case of those descended from enslaved peoples, reconstructing cultural memory in the African diaspora. This chapter examines both expressions of memory, as horror and as healing, in the speculative fiction of Black women, countering narratives of trauma and loss at the societal and interpersonal levels.

Familial and ancestral relationships are often the site of scholarly inquiry in Black women's literature. Relationships between mothers and daughters and the matrilineal presence have been studied at length by scholars such as Patricia Hill Collins and Simone A. James Alexander. These scholars often examined Black women's writing as counter-narratives to the mainstream US narratives surrounding pathologized Black motherhood stemming from, in part, the notorious Moynihan Report condemning Black mothers, suggesting their supposedly inappropriate modeling of masculine, self-sufficient femininity contributed to the decline of the Black American family and a destructive culture resulting in inescapable poverty. Of course, this narrative of pathology does not begin with the report, but rather emerges alongside chattel slavery in the US, where Black women were considered "natally dead" in that they were legally and socially considered to have no relationship with either their parents or their progeny (Patton 3). The strength and resilience employed by Black women to resist these destructive narratives was further pathologized by the reigning anti-Blackness. Hortense Spillers notes how this problematic notion creeps into both Black and white scholars' criticism of Black women, "the African-American female's 'dominance' and 'strength' come to be interpreted by later generations—both black and white, oddly enough—as a 'pathology,' as an instrument of castration" (Spillers 74). However, Black women's literature serves as a means through which counter-narratives are deployed. The emphasis on family so frequently found in Black women's literature rejects the enduring notion of Black women as being "somehow disconnected from the progeny of their wombs," restoring and exploring lineage and familial relationships (Patton 3).

Familial connection among the living is but one facet of this counter-narrative. The ancestral is equally important in Black women's writing as an act of reconstructing familial and cultural histories lost under chattel slavery in the Black Atlantic. As Holloway notes: "The ancestral presence constitutes the posture of (re)membrance. She is the linking of gender and culture that pulls these writers' works together. She accomplishes mediation in the connection of her figurative and metaphorical presence to the textual strategies of (re)membrance, revision, and recursion" (15). The limited scholarly discussion of genre, however, minimizes the rhetorical work of these authors. Because these storytelling strategies exist in the realm of science fiction or fantasy, they are dismissed as generic conventions, which Toni Morrison argues "for literary historians and literary critics [magical realism] just seemed to be a convenient way to skip again what was the truth in the art of certain writers" (qtd. in McGregory 414). The dismissive approach to genre writing equally limits our ability to understand the power of the speculative as writing that allows free association rendering the cultural presence of the ancestor and cultural memory concrete. Examining these strategies not simply as rhetorical device or clever writing style, interrogating the speculative as a "legitimate" means of expressing desire for change requires moving beyond an interrogation of the genre and generic elements to examine how these moves reflect similar aims and concerns of Black women's literature, meeting Morrison's own call for an instructive Black literature that reveals threats to the community (Morrison, "Rootedness" 58–59).

Memory as Trauma/Horror

The call to reconstruct seemingly lost histories within the African diaspora extends to cultural memory that is equally forward-looking while it attempts to reconstitute the past. As Okpalaoka notes, "cultural memory is . . . not a phenomenon that is exclusively limited to our past experiences but is one that points toward a future present in which African ascendant people are agents in the continuous creation of new memories from old ones" (Okpalaoka 88). Indeed, cultural memory is one that helps us to understand not only who we were, but who we are.

As a subset of the notion of cultural memory, trauma studies began with the examination of the Holocaust as a trauma central to modern Jewish identity that continues to shape responses to the world. Chattel slavery equally provides a central trauma for the Black Atlantic that shapes not only our responses to the world, but also the world's responses to us. Toni Morrison shapes the notion of the intrusive thought into rememory, or particularly strong memories that recur, things that cannot be forgotten. *Beloved* uses rememory in relationship to Sethe whose traumatic murder of her child to protect her returns so strongly that it manifests in a haunting presence and an embodied visitor to their home (Morrison, *Beloved*). This is a speculative version of the classic model of trauma according to Caruth where trauma is expressed via the "literal return of the event against the will of the one it inhabits" (Caruth 5). Psychoanalytic feminists have also linked this notion to the idea of the return of the repressed or to Julia Kristeva's abjection, that which cannot be expelled even though it disgusts and shames us.

However, rememory is not just shame that cannot be escaped or a recurring and intrusive thought; it also holds the power to transform trauma. Virginia Hamilton expressed rememory as "'reword . . . a volunteer, like a self-sown seed come forth unbidden'" (Wallace). Remembering her grandfather's fist, burned closed after a gunpowder factory accident, Hamilton describes wrapping her hands around it as he swung her around with strength. The closed fist with magic inside came to be a myth and a powerful source of rememory for the author, a way of reclaiming and reenvisioning a traumatic event in the life of her grandfather, recasting it as a powerful expression of her grandfather's love. This is typical of Black writers, according to Pin-chia Feng. Feng notes that Afro-Caribbean writers frequently employ folk rituals of rememory as a method for "spiritual and psychological healing" (Feng 150). Storytelling within this tradition "aim[s] to exorcise sources of evil from both within and outside of the community." Susana M. Morris extends this to Afrofuturism providing a definition of the term as "a framework for Black joy [or] a way to move into the future, situating and framing Black joy" (Morris, "Black Women"). Rememory, representative of at once an unforgettable trauma and a present joy all cast into the future, is a central means by which Black women express memory through the speculative.

Taken together we can see Black women's powerful interpretation of memory as a means of recasting trauma, emphasizing love over and against pain. It also confronts the notion that forgetting even painful events can often also mean letting go of the sources of love and power that Black people need to survive in an anti-Black world. Remembering with an emphasis on love strengthens community connections, not only clearing a path to move forward toward interpersonal and familial healing but equally highlighting larger dangers to the community. The doubled function of traumatic memory as both horror and healing occurs in different generic permutations across Tananarive Due's *The Good House* and Nalo Hopkinson's *The New Moon's Arms*. *The Good House* tells the tale of a conjure woman who attempts to protect her family from vengeful spirits by taking her knowledge of rootwork to the grave. This attempt fails spectacularly, leaving both her family and the larger community vulnerable to the spirit's assault. The horror is only resolved by reaching beyond the veil of life and death to transmit knowledge and restore familial and cultural memory.

Equally featuring traumatic memory as horror and healing, *The New Moon's Arms* centers a Caribbean woman nearing menopause whose hot flashes manifest items and memories from her past. As she confronts her own past trauma and the history of slavery in her fictional island community, she heals relationships with her daughter and former circle of friends while working to end the pollution of their island and its waters. In each of these stories, Black remembrance creates rootedness, allowing the protagonists to draw on ancestral wisdom to address looming threats, be they physical violence, the pollution of the waters, or the spiritual poisoning of a community.

The Horror and Healing of Remembrance in *The Good House*

Haunting often represents tormented histories that refuse to be forgotten, that reemerge despite one's best attempts at suppression. Studies of Gayl Jones's *Corregidora* suggest that "rememory acts as a haunting presence, a form of memory and a practice of remembrance that haunts those who remember" (Setka, "Haunted" 131). However, practices of remembrance within the horror genre also lend themselves to celebration, as well as the reconstruction and reclamation of strength from cultural history. This is particularly visible in novels that weave together African-influenced folklore with Westernized genres of horror, fantasy, and science fiction creating a genre that Kinitra D. Brooks refers to as "folkloric horror" (98). Using this genre to "tap into the power" of ancestral wisdom (Patton), remembrance realized in Black women's speculative literature shifts representation of spiritual possession from the demonic as represented in mainstream film and literature to a legitimate spiritual experience, celebrating knowledge systems grounded in African-inspired cosmologies such as Vodou and Santeria, and espousing "the black spiritual feminine to achieve a revised literary articulation of the Mambo, the Santera, and the Obeah woman" (Brooks 103). This remembrance refuses the history of white American horror tales that cast African-inspired spiritual practices, such as possession, as inherently evil, treating them rather as "valued ontology and valued epistemological tool[s]" (Brooks 103). In this way, the elements of horror lay not in the practice or the memory of African-derived spiritual practices but rather in the loss of connection to the past, reflecting the trauma of colonization, slavery, and the erasure of Black history in the Western world as the source of horror. This reflection can be seen clearly in Tananarive Due's *The Good House*. As an example of folkloric horror, the breakdown of ancestral knowledge in the novel unleashes the terrifying forces of demonic destruction at work in the lives of the Toussaint family.

The nonlinear narrative of *The Good House* jumps between characters and time periods in the lives of the Toussaint family. Grandma Marie's story begins in the 1920s, when she is grappling with her spiritual power, jumping to her grandson Corey's suicide in the summer of 2000, and finally the aftermath of that supposed suicide for Corey's mother Angela and her ex-husband Tariq in 2001. Called back to site of that tragic summer to sell her grandmother's estate, known as the Good House, Angela sits at the center of a storm as several townspeople either kill themselves or commit murder-suicide seemingly out of nowhere. To defeat the growing threat, Angela must first uncover the truth of her family's history and come to believe in Grandma Marie's power. This element of nonlinear temporality, further discussed in chapter 3 and commonly used in literature and film, disrupts the notion of haunting as repressed trauma. The ancestors are continuously present, simply abiding on another plane of existence. The "ghosts" of the haunted house are not destructive forces seeking to cause harm or relive their own trauma but serve as reserves of power and knowledge trying to restore the transmission of ancestral knowledge. *The Good House* is a story rooted in the past and the mistakes made during that time, while also exploring the consequences of those previous actions in the narrative's present and altering the future. That the ancestors have a vantage point beyond linear time that allows them to see this expanded sense of time, where past, present, and future happen at once, is one of the key features of Afrofuturist texts.

The novel equally shifts the haunted house narrative from the house itself to a story of the land, reflecting African-derived religious beliefs. "In a traditional Vodou view, the land, the family, and the spirits are, in a way, one and the same" (Brown, *Mama Lola* 36). Drawn to the energy of land on which the Good House sits, Marie's story hinges on a moment of hubris during which she violates this sacred space and her relationship with Papa Legbas, the keeper of the crossroads. In doing so, she unleashes a *baka*, an evil spirit who possesses and drains the life force of those around Marie, seeking to destroy Marie's entire family line for her prideful actions. After the spirit possesses a young white girl in her small town, Marie precariously casts the spirit out. Believing she has subdued the baka, she finds her own daughter has been possessed and driven mad by the voice of the baka. Feeling guilty for the harm Marie has caused and in a misguided attempt to save her granddaughter, Angela, Marie refuses to pass on the knowledge to Angela, or her great-grandson, Corey, who was quite young at the time of Marie's passing. Marie stops Angela from dreaming, in order to hide her from the baka. However, Marie's attempts to subdue the baka are superficial and this refusal to pass this knowledge on is the key factor in the horrific events to come.

As the baka continues to haunt the margins of the land, teenage Corey visits the house for the first time since Grandma Marie's death and begins to have dreams of the door where Grandma Marie's diary and spellbook is hidden from the baka. As a driving narrative device, dreams form the conduit through which those in the spiritual realm can communicate with the physical realm, as Corey's friend Sean tells him, while urging him to open the door: "Well, what are you waiting for? Dreams are messages, dude" (179). What the two never consider is who is sending the messages and their intent in doing so. Although Corey is not aware of his family's power, he remains vulnerable to those who are. That this lost legacy serves as the beginning of the horror story suggests that when we do not share our histories, they are told to us by forces that do not have our best interests at heart.

Marie's refusal of her role as familial and communal elder compounds her violation of the sacred land. As Patton notes, "elders serve as conduits of ancestral wisdom through their role as culture bearers because they pass down the wisdom of the ancestors" (31). Elder status is not achieved by simply aging, "but [is] an accomplishment dependent on drawing on the wisdom of the ancestors" (Patton 31). Marie's refusal to pass on ancestral knowledge ultimately endangers her entire familial line. Indeed, her rejection of the role of culture-bearer within her own family has an impact that reaches far beyond the family. The harm of forgetting this wisdom spills out into the entire community, killing innocent and guilty alike. Among the baka's victims are townspeople, including the neighbor who adopts mistreated children providing necessary stability in their lives, a man who is aware and respectful of Native American history in the area. His loss further deprives the community of an elder possessing specific and useful knowledge. Another community member murders his son and then kills himself. Anyone who knows any piece of Marie's history is targeted by the baka in an effort to weaken her ability to fight back. The baka's power grows as the ability to access ancestral memory is diminished. The crux of the novel's tension lies in the failure to act appropriately as an elder and transmit ancestral knowledge, suggesting that to fail as a conduit in the transmission of cultural history is to enact violence not only toward one's own family but the community at large. To forget in this context reenacts the horror of the construction of enslaved Black women as natally dead, incapable of familial relationships, reduced to a lone individual.

In this way, Due renders the failure to remember as an act of horror, highlighting familial and cultural memory as necessary for survival to both one's familial line extending both forward and backward through time and the health of the community. Providing a site for counter-narrative, the speculative novel's connected nature of family members both living and dead within Marie and Angela's family and the relationship to land and stewardship of a sacred site recognized both by Indigenous and Black rootworkers, as well as the connection of the larger community, challenge individualist horror narratives such as *Candyman* where one protects oneself by simply walking away, disconnecting from larger community concerns. By rejecting the cultural narrative of pathological Black matriarchy, Due posits Black maternal figures not as the illness but rather as the cure to her family's trauma. Due's novel equally reflects restorative fabulation as it reckons with an initial trauma that cannot be changed in Marie's violation of her spiritual power. It does not seek to change what cannot be altered but recognizes that communication and the careful transmission of cultural memory provides a source of power and agency in generations to come. As an emotional balm for the reader, the narrative provides a frame for understanding how to deal with harm we have caused, moving forward to remember both the pain and the larger cultural memory that carries with it resistance, agency, and power.

While forgetting is the root cause of the horrific events of *The Good House* and, to a lesser extent, the moments of terror within *The New Moon's Arms*, remembering is the balm for the community, the protagonists' families, and even their own bodies in several important ways. The transformative power of rememory reshapes painful traumas into deep expressions of cultural, familial, and self love. The practice of conjure in Black women's speculative fiction is a powerful means of the reclamation of legacies that have been stigmatized, diminished, or erased by racist colonial practices and equally reinforced by internalized racist practices of Black folks in the storytelling of

Black women. Kameelah L. Martin contends that African American women use the conjure woman as means to achieve "rituals of rememory" that heal cultural trauma. Vodou has long been demonized within the US both in literature, film, and television. Beginning as part of American's understanding of the success of the Haitian revolution as a pact with the devil and continuing as justification for the exclusion and/or exploitation of the Afro-Caribbean, Martin traces the positive representation of the Black priestess in Black literature to folktales of conjure women who employed their spiritual powers to overcome threats to the physical, social, and psychological well-being of an individual (Martin, *Envisioning* xxi). Transformed into folk heroes, these characters of conjure tales were able to exist outside of the power of the system of slavery; wielded the power to combat illness; promoted harmony in the social lives of Black people; provided protection from theft, physical, or spiritual harm; and demonstrated agency through exemplifying a source of power available to Black people to shape the forces around them, offering a pathway for connecting with African history and spirituality (Martin, *Conjuring* 15).

Due's vision of conjure dovetails with Martin's notion of the Black priestess as an empowering image of Black spiritual womanhood. While Martin defines her initially as a controlling image that maligns Black women engaged in spirit work, Martin hopes for a safe representational space that allows the priestess to be an active subject rather than passive object, empowered by Black folk tradition, and with agency to make decisions concerning her immediate circumstances. The role of spiritual possession in *The Good House* contributes to a shift in the Black priestess. Whereas typical mainstream depictions of Vodou suggest that spiritual possession is inherently evil, possession in the novel is simply a tool to be used for good or evil employed both by the baka and the protagonists. When used for good, it represents giving oneself over to memory. Through this communal contact with the ancestral, the possessed Angela accesses lost knowledge and represents the only way to defeat the baka.

> *It's happening now. I'm losing myself now,* she thought, and she went rigid. This felt like bedtime all over again, when she slowly surrendered to sleep and jumped to wakefulness as soon as she slipped into new territory, into places that scared her. She ran from the memories. She always ran. But she would not run now. She could not. With a deep sigh, finding strength in the scents of cedar and fir around her, Angela closed her eyes. And she slipped, as if through a hole in her mind. A low hum surrounded her; not a machine's hum, but a hum that sounded like a chorus of human voices in soft unison." (432–33).

The possession is initially presented as a terrifying loss of self, but as the hum of voices rises, it ultimately becomes a healing and connective gift of love from departed family members. By letting go of her individuality, Angela becomes connected to ancestral memory and the knowledge and confidence necessary to defeat the evil spirit seeking to destroy her family. In this way, Due's tale rewrites the role of possession from a source of evil, allying one with the powers of darkness, to a source of communion rooted in Afro-diasporic history and cultures and represents the Black priestess as powerful matriarchal role of culture-bearing, passing knowledge from one generation to the next, preserving not only one's family but also the health of the community at large.

In addition to familial history, among the functions of memory in *The Good House* is the role of supplying strength for the fight against evil. Tariq's internal battle with the baka speaks to the importance of cultural memory as a source of resilience. Although Tariq eventually succumbs to the baka's power, he resists for over a year before losing his final battle, finding pools of inner strength the others killed by the baka do not possess. The reader's introduction to the character suggests that Tariq's inner strength has its origins in maintaining strong connections to the Black community and the resources of cultural memory therein. The Marcus Bookstore, a Black-owned bookstore that Tariq visits, provides his connection with community, cultural history, and spiritual memory. As Tariq remarks, "Marcus was the medicine a doctor couldn't give him" (Due 193). The baka's spiritual attack centers on Tariq's stomach and he finds himself emanating a smell that he cannot wash off. Although he has seen multiple specialists seeking a cure, Tariq found the healing balm of Black intellectual thought and artistic expression that literally fed his soul as the baka attempted to destroy it: "His discoveries at Marcus were feeding him, and there were times he felt almost whole again. Brief, glorious times" (194). Via his connection to the bookstore, he read biographies and found an interest in fiction, even reading science fiction written by Black authors and realizing the depths to which he had been indoctrinated in a limited vision of Blackness: "He hadn't known there were any black folks in outer space, not from the movies and books he'd seen when he was a kid. That was news to him" (194). Although Tariq ultimately succumbs to the baka's attack, he withstands the attack for nearly a year, much longer than the minutes or days that fell the others. The knowledge Tariq obtains, and his expanded definition of Blackness, inform his ability to withstand the struggle for his soul, providing brief moments of glorious wholeness, suggesting that this form of self-love, that is, the recognition of recorded history and cultural memory found in historical texts—literature, and artwork—are restorative and sustaining elements. As Tariq consumes Afro-diasporic history and culture, he finds himself further steeled against spiritual attack. By learning, Tariq rewrites his own narrative as well, coming to understand how limited constructions of Blackness had shaped his life and the possibilities he considered available to himself. Learning this history and consuming this artwork offers means to restoratively fabulate his life, to open possibilities for himself and others in his world. This contact inures him to spiritual attack, offering critical confidence in himself and his cultural history.

Although sustaining power expands beyond the spiritual in the cultural memory of the bookstore, spirituality equally offers respite. Tariq's bookstore visits bring him contact with Afro-religiosity that could help him banish the baka. Reflecting that Afro-religiosity is itself an attempt to "heal the traumatic disunion" from Africa by peoples across the African diaspora (Martin 23), Tariq's last opportunity to save himself occurs at the bookstore in an encounter with Brother Paul, an author, poet, and healer knowledgeable not just in Caribbean politics and society, but in Afro-diasporic rootwork and healing practices. Brother Paul recognizes the smell emanating from Tariq and the imminent danger that threatens him, reminding Tariq that he had offered his help before and was offering it once again. Unfortunately, under the influence of the baka who plays on Tariq's suspicion of Paul's theories, Tariq dismisses him. "The brother was pretty far out there, telling him he should look for a new underground drug supposedly made from African blood, or some such pitiful Afrocentric horseshit. Tariq was surprised he'd forgotten a conversation like that, but he'd been doing that a lot lately. Forgetting things, like he had when his face was buried in coke" (195). This exchange is important in a number of ways. The baka inflames Tariq's own internalized anti-Blackness, the very anti-Blackness that had been challenged by his increasing familiarity of Black history, referring to Paul's spiritual advice as "Afrocentric horseshit." The baka equally highlights the power of ancestral knowledge, causing Tariq to not just dismiss the contents of the conversation, but to forget the conversation ever took place. In doing so, we come to understand the healing power of cultural and spiritual memory as well as the horror of forgetting.

Paul represents the presence of this ancestral wisdom, tracing his own ability back to his Trinidadian aunt, who taught him to prepare herbs and read Tarot cards. Despite Tariq's interest in receiving help, the baka equally plays on Tariq's existing homophobia, flaring it into a burning desire to hurt Brother Paul. Accusing him of desiring time alone for sex, Tariq's inability to overcome this homophobia marks his final moments of resistance. Using internalized hatred to successfully block Tariq from accessing cultural memory, the baka claims his soul and puts Tariq's body to use for his own violent ends. The story challenges toxic masculinity in two remarkable ways. First, the transmission of cultural memory through Paul's aunt notes the recognition of matriarchal authority and role of Black women as culture bearers. Second, Tariq's homophobic rant built on a hatred of the potential femininity of gay men is a marker of his demise. Had Tariq been able to combat his own internalized toxic masculinity and take advice from Brother Paul, he might have been able to save himself from the baka. This potential strengthened connection to community and ancestral wisdom also marks a missed opportunity to recruit an ally in the fight to not only banish the baka, but to return his son Cory to the plane of the living. Toxic masculinity is exposed as a limiting diversion of Black spiritual power and as ultimately a threat to the very life of Tariq's own son. Indeed, one marker of Tariq's affliction is his rejection of the healer and the community Paul offers. Not only has Tariq's strength and ability to fight the baka come from his engagement with community, so too does the final battle for his soul end with Tariq's rejection of that same community's help.

Memory equally holds the power to render justice for generational wrongs or violations. The land had long been a sacred site recognized by multiple cultures for its power. Indeed, even after Marie's violation of her powers, the land continued to produce herbs of unusual potency, even growing out of season (Due 66). Marie's partner John, an Indigenous man from the region, noted that his people were buried there. Angela Toussaint, while possessed by her grandmother and able to see between the planes of existence, saw canoes hanging from the trees. "The canoes were the last remnants of a people, and their spirits had been there all along, whispering stories as they hung" (Due 458). As an ancient site of power, it was the place from which the baka emerged and the site of the final battle to remove it from the human plane. Although Marie had violated the land in search of power and revenge during her own lifetime, the continued impact can be felt three generations later, a truth about generational trauma well-known in the Black community. While the plants continued to grow without issue, the markers of generational trauma were present in the animals of the area. Ravens flocked to the area, watching human trespassers with suspicion.

> The ravens on this property were goddamned possessive, chattering at him as if they expected him to pay a toll. [The ravens sat on a nearby tree branch] . . . all three of them regarding him with a convincing imitation of intelligence. Their black eyes were unblinking, appearing to follow his

movements. Weird. He couldn't think of a single time he'd come out here when the ravens didn't gather around the garden to watch him. Still, he couldn't spot their nests. (65–67)

Remembrance heals the animosity and violation of the land. Just as this violation has generational impact, so too does the restoration of the relationship with Papa Legbas. As Angela completes her task, destroying the baka, she is met by her ancestors holding a great celebration. Angela's mother, tormented her entire life by the baka until driven to suicide, is returned to her childhood self. Marie also congratulates Angela for her bravery and offers her a wish. Her seemingly impossible wish is that Cory be returned to life. As a reward, she is returned to the summer of Cory's apparent suicide and through communication with her son is able to save his life as well as the lives of all the townspeople through whom the baka had wrought his wrath.

The land and the people are as deeply intertwined as the past, present, and future. As she made her way through the woods toward the sound of the celebration, her connection to the ancestors became more tangible. "The memories made Angela dizzy, gathering strength with the beating rain. These new memories were the ones closest to the surface, the ones tethered to her and Gramma Marie. These woods were a haven for spirits, and spirits lived on memories" (423). The strongest spiritual power of the land, named The Spot by local teenagers. As the various planes of existence collapse, so too does time contract, uniting past and future into a singular moment. "To Angela, from the moment she walked to the center of The Spot, time became a fog. Seconds and minutes became indistinguishable to her. Only one moment mattered: *Now*. Her future depended on it. Much more than that depended on it" (Due 431).

Generations of ancestors gathered in The Spot to celebrate the restoration of the land, the defeat of the baka, and the reconciliation of the family with the *lwas*. The description of this otherworldly plane differs from visions of Christian heaven as typically depicted as a literally white space, white clouds, white robes, white angels, and ultimately a white, male god. Due's version of the space of the ancestors is quite terrestrial, a blend of Native Americans, Africans, African Americans, and a few white people. Rather than a vision of Christian heaven, we see another plane of existence that is rooted in Afro-religious practices. "See how we're blessed with the favor of the lwas? We are no longer exiled. But that's the start, not the finish. God is smiling on us. This is a miracle day" (Due 461). In this place, Angela feels a fog descend over her most recent memories of trauma in her fight with Tariq/the baka and she connects with ancestral memory and love. Ancestral memory eases the emotional and physical pain of this particular fight, and using the speculative takes this healing a step further to physically rewrite the world, restoring Corey and all those killed by the baka to life.

The path to this healing arrived in a combination of remembering and accepting or belief in the ancestral memory over and against the Western world's perception of reality. Angela struggled throughout the narrative to believe what she was experiencing, to believe in the existence of the baka, and had to be persuaded to believe in a miracle as well. In an interstitial page titled "Miracle," Due uses a biblical passage from Luke and a West African proverb to introduce the miracle—a second chance. This move blending Christian and West African thought reflects the continuing Afro-religiosity, itself a blend of West African traditional religions, Native American religions, and Christian beliefs. The passage from Luke 7:14–15, "And he said, Young man, I say unto thee, Arise. And he that was dead sat up and began to speak. And he delivered him to his mother." The West African proverb, "Where there is mud, there must be water" notes the shift in perspective necessary to transform trauma as in rememory. These two thoughts are blended, pointing toward the possibility of redemption and reward at the end of struggle. Indeed, divine reward for the pain of suffering has been a staple of Black American Christian religious thought. It helped enslaved people survive servitude, offered emotional support during Jim Crow, and continues to be a strong thread within the Black American Christian tradition.

Angela's second chance with Corey is to connect and listen to him, listen to herself about what she really wants in her romantic relationship with Tariq, to reconnect to family and the present. This is facilitated by her reconnection with ancestral history and the healing of historic spiritual wounds. As she rewrites the immediate history as a reward for spiritual restoration of the family's favor with Papa Legba, the effects spill out into the larger community preventing the deaths of several town members in addition to those of Corey and Tariq.

The Healing and Horror of Memory in *The New Moon's Arms*

The loss of cultural and familial memory is represented as equally traumatic in Nalo Hopkinson's *The New Moon's Arms*. Turning from horror toward fantasy, *The New Moon's Arms* resists genre categorization. Characterizing her own work as speculative fiction, Hopkinson allows for the inclusion of elements of science fiction, fantasy, dark fantasy, horror, and magical realism (Hopkinson). While the explicit horror of an evil spirit terrorizing a family and an entire community represents the horrors of the loss of cultural memory in *The Good House*, *The New Moon's Arms* shifts the horror to repressed memory that can no longer be denied. Just as the restoration of familial memory ends the horror facing that community in Tananarive Due's text, Hopkinson's protagonist resolves her story by integrating her own past events, both familial and cultural, including the uncertainties of the unresolved mystery of her mother's disappearance. In this novel, the rememory as intrusive thought, as defined by Toni Morrison, shifts to the rememory of Virginia Hamilton, where the traumatic is fully integrated and allowed to exist in all its complexity, equally finding room for pain, grief, and joy.

The New Moon's Arms is the story of Calamity Lambkin, a perimenopausal single mother, facing the recent death of her father, a distant relationship with her own adult daughter and grandson, and the arrival of a young boy found washed up on the beach next to a strange dead woman. As she cares for the child, she relives and rediscovers her past, transforming her relationships with family, friends, lovers, and the land itself. Just as the horror in *The Good House* emerges from the failure to share history and the repression of familial memory, so too does the horror in Calamity's story spring from forgetting and a refusal to act as an elder for one's community. Although Calamity had worked to repress the memories of her youth and the pain of her mother's disappearance, as well as her own fear of growing older, her hot flashes and the undeniable hormonal changes in her body as Calamity approaches menopause connect her to a force that will not be repressed. Calamity's rememory renders the past tangible as objects such as plates, small toys, or photographs appear around her with each hot flash, the most shocking of which is the sudden appearance of a complete dwarf-cashew grove from her childhood home that had been long lost to a hurricane's rising waters.

Calamity's childhood home was on an island named Blessée, a false English cognate that sounds and looks to the English-speaking eye to mean "blessed." However, the English translation from French is "injured." This doubled meaning, at once injured and blessed, mirrors both the history of the island as a site of brutality, destruction, and survival as well as Calamity's internal state of denial and recovery. By juxtaposing these two terms, I resist invoking the thread of thought among the culture of toxic positivity that everything happens for a reason that must certainly be for the best or that the history of colonization and trans-Atlantic slavery was a positive occurrence. This thinking is often used to paper over "negative" emotions characterizing grief, anger, and pain as both avoidable and undesirable. Rather, I want to highlight the notion of rememory as tool used to transform trauma into healing and restorative fabulation that both acknowledges a past that cannot be altered while examining how we might move forward from that trauma without requiring it be buried or forgotten. Calamity reflects this duality, both by changing her name from Chastity to Calamity and considering herself blessed in her arrogance and demand to control others' lives, but secretly quite injured emotionally by the way she was raised and the emotional injuries of her youth. Via remembrance, her emotional wounds begin to heal, and Calamity is able to understand how her actions emerging from that buried trauma have, in turn, harmed all of her familial, platonic, and romantic relationships, alienating each person with her gendered and homophobic judgments of their lives.

Calamity's traumas and the responses they engender are active along multiple axes, most notably bodily autonomy, sexuality, and generational repression. Calamity was not permitted to explore or experience her body while growing up. The nakedness she enjoyed as a child was met with shame from her family. As a teenager, Calamity's sexual explorations ended with pregnancy and resulting expulsion from her father's home. However, her sexual exploration was driven from a place of both internal desire and budding sexuality, as well as rooted in compulsory heterosexuality and the homophobia of her Christian upbringing. Having sex with her best friend Michael was meant to save him from his stated desire for male bodies, both seeing him as a problem to be fixed and transforming her body into a tool or a vessel through which the patriarchal power of compulsory heterosexuality moves. Calamity equally expresses homophobia when Hector, her new lover, reveals he is bisexual. In a painful exchange, Calamity impugns Hector's masculinity, relying on compulsory heterosexuality and toxic masculinity to define "real" manhood and Hector's lack thereof. A second exchange with Michael's partner, Orso, when he volunteers to watch Agway while Calamity goes on a date, reveals Calamity's belief that gay men prey on children. These extremely hurtful and inaccurate ideas mirror the ways Calamity was rejected for her own "inappropriately" expressed heterosexuality. Healing trauma in this case looks like understanding that ways in which she is perpetuating the pain she received and directing her hurt toward others rather than interrogating the root cause.

Calamity spends the rest of her life moving in response to the early messages as appropriate (hetero)sexuality, challenging them by embracing her skin and sexual desires. Unfortunately, in turn, Calamity limits the bodily autonomy of others in her circle. Discovering a young boy washed up on the beach, whom she names Agway after a sound he makes that she calls unintelligible "babble," Calamity feels a kinship with him and takes him in. The young boy has long hair with shells woven into it which she finds untidy and decides to cut his hair, which deeply upsets him. Calamity gives in to pressure to surgically alter his body, removing the rough patches of tacky skin on the insides of his knees that allow him to press his legs together to swim more effectively and erasing the evolutionary adaptations the merpeople have made to live in the sea. Calamity's refusal of Agway's bodily autonomy speaks again to her desire to repress the possibility of uncomfortable truths about the boy and her own history. This equally represents the larger destructive desire to erase uncomfortable histories and how that destructive desire is enacted on the bodies of those least able politically to speak for themselves, enacting a horror of erasure upon those bodies. Despite her alteration of the young boy's body in an effort to suppress these truths, Calamity's own body does not forget and refuses to allow her to repress the passage of time. Her hot flashes, signally oncoming menopause, are a mechanism of bodily memory that ultimately reminds her of how the body holds memory. In addition to physical scars, bodily memory is represented in genetic adaptations, such as the merpeople's knee skin.

Calamity's refusal of other's bodily autonomy reflects her own state of disconnection from her body. Much of Calamity's journey in the novel is recovering her bodily sensations, particularly her ability to "find" that returns with the onset of menopause and learning to trust them rather than deny them. Perhaps more importantly, she learns to trust her memories and experiences that others had tried to deny. Calamity and the "dada-hair lady," an African traditional religious leader sold into slavery and brought to the Caribbean whose story is told in a flashback, share the same "finding" ability. Calamity's two fingers on her left hand are fused at the lowest joint and often itch just before one of these objects from the past manifests in her presence. While Calamity had had this power as a young girl, it was not nearly as strong. She sensed where to look to find lost objects rather than them appearing before her as they would later in life. She blocked this ability when her mother disappeared, knowing that she had likely drowned in the sea and not wanting to find her bloated corpse. Although she had buried this ability and the painful memories associated with its end, her body remembers its ability and history, overriding her attempts at suppression.

This link between body, memory, and sensation is borne out in medical trauma studies. Indeed, just as Calamity's girlhood trauma taught her to become partially insensate, losing her ability to "find" with the tingle in her fingers, so too do real-world survivors of childhood trauma often lose sensation, often feeling partial numbness. "Sometimes we use our bodies not to discover facts, but to hide them. . . . One of the things the screen hides most effectively is the body, our own body, by which I mean the ins of it, the interiors. Like a veil thrown over the skin to secure its modesty, the screen partially removes from the mind the inner states of the body, those that constitute the flow of life as it wanders in the journey of each day" (Damasio qtd. in Van der Kolk, *Body*). Survivors "often become expert at ignoring their gut feelings and in numbing awareness of what is played out inside. They learn to hide from their selves" (Van der Kolk 154). It is only by reconnecting to these sensations can one heal and end the repetitive trauma cycle. "If you have a comfortable connection with your inner sensations—if you can trust them to give you accurate information—you will feel in charge of your body, your feelings, and your self" (Van der Kolk 154). Indeed, learning to trust her body and believe what it is telling her despite the cultural messages of impossibility forms a significant piece of Calamity's ability to accept her role as matriarch and rebuild long-term relationships.

Calamity's story demonstrates how the Black body functions as a site of cultural inscription, how Black history is written on the body, trauma housed in the body and the ways that it emerges, as well as bodily autonomy versus the political will to control the body via the erasure of bodies and histories. The stories of merpeople are relegated to folklore and hushed whispers among those who work near the sea in the novel. Most of the island archipelago continues to operate in a world in which mermaids mean only white women with "tea-cup breasts," rather than the reality of their world in which the sea-people are both real and have a complex history that unites the forced migration of Africans to the island during the Trans-Atlantic slave trade; their refusal to cooperate, instead choosing to walk into the sea; the combined European and African folklore of selkies and Mami Wata; and the monk seals of the island who present a genetic mystery as they are Mediterranean in origin, rather than Caribbean, and the threat to their habitat caused by the environmental destruction of the archipelago's natural resources. This erasure of history and culture reflected in the representation of mermaids as white women equally represents an erasure of the bodies of the merpeople and any coinciding recognition of their lives and homes as a necessary site of environmental protection. However, the novel flashes back to the past following the story of the dada-hair lady, a woman we find to be an enslaved African woman on a ship to the Caribbean. As they near the land, she calls on Mami Wata and the power of her menstruation to save the Africans aboard the ship. Transforming into monk seals, they dive into the water to become a community of monk seals and merpeople. In this moment of transformation, we see a bodily inscription other than scar tissue as history of Black bodies is so often depicted. The enslaved people's bodies shift into an entirely new form, escaping the control of enslavers and achieving ultimate freedom. Indeed, even as monk seals, they cannot be contained in the zoo aquarium. They frequently leave and return to their artificial habitat to the constant bafflement and frustration of zookeepers. They live to preserve their history and cultural memory in a new form.

In a clever and complex turn, we equally understand the deep connections between human life, monk seals, the history of the trans-Atlantic slave trade, and the current-day pollution of the waters off the coast of the archipelago. The international-business-friendly politicians have allowed a salt manufacturing company to build factories and dump waste illegally in the waters around the islands, causing a drop in fish populations that feed the monk seals, merpeople populations, and the food supply of humans on the island, while also impacting the small-scale salt farmers and fishermen who derive their living from the local waters. We cannot simply dismiss animal life as less than human and undeserving of protection. In fact, animal and human lives are deeply entwined in the story, calling attention to the desire both to dismiss animal life and to dismiss Black life as disposable.

At work is also the notion that Calamity must relearn to trust her own memories despite how others try to shape her experiences. This cultural trauma emerging from both history and memory is shaped by larger forces of colonization, white supremacy, and Black cultural memory and is equally shaped at the individual level by her family members who refuse to listen to Calamity's experience meeting the young sea girl who invited Calamity to swim beyond her capability and saved her by returning her to shore after Calamity injured herself. Although Calamity has lived her life in response to that denial of her own experience, she in turn brings this generational trauma to her own child and grandchild by attempting to force their bodies and memories into a shape that she desires. When she can validate her own experiences and memories, as recalled to her by her own body, she can begin to unpack the larger ways in which she has passed that trauma forward. Her relationship with her family is a microcosm of the larger cultural trauma colonization has wrought on the island and the community living on it.

The refusal to acknowledge the past extends to Calamity's equal refusal of her role as an elder in the community. Calamity's emotional stuntedness is largely connected to the ways in which she felt she was denied a childhood and has spent the latter years of her life attempting to recapture this time. While the rare depictions of women experiencing Peter Pan syndrome are simply written off as failed women, terrible mothers, or uncaring and selfish women, Hopkinson's depiction of Calamity is much more forgiving. Hopkinson's treatment of Calamity recognizes that she lost her mother while very young, under mysterious circumstances that altered her relationship with her father and sent her searching for connection with her friend and future father of her child. The resulting pregnancy and her shame-filled expulsion from her family home and larger community forced Calamity to adulthood responsibility well before her time. As she aged and her daughter moved away from home, Calamity responded by returning to her sense of childhood, refusing to acknowledge her age, not wanting to be seen as a mother or grandmother, and refusing the signs of her own body. However, her attempts to relive her youth have had damaging effects on her relationship with her family and friends. As a result, Calamity does not wish to make long-lasting connections of any type, romantic or familial.

Calamity moves toward acceptance of her role via remembrance and through developing caring relationships. As Anatol notes, "taking on the nurturing of a child left on the beach . . . allows the protagonist and the people in her life to re-evaluate their narrow conceptions of what makes a 'good' and 'good' mother" (Anatol 202). Indeed, this challenge to the binary of good or bad mother equally extends to Calamity's perception of "matriarch" as an old and sexually undesirable woman. By embracing her traumatic history and healing relationships with her daughter and with Michael and his partner, Orso, and returning Agway to his family of sea-people and begging forgiveness for his altered body, she begins to understand that what she had previously determined to be disastrous or calamitous approach to life did not to define her and that she could define "matriarch" however she wanted. Just as Schreiber notes "communal rememory transforms traumatic personal memory," as she rejoins her community, reconnecting with her childhood friend and family, the communal rememory of her own life experiences transform her own traumatic history into a story that helps her heal (43).

The fantastic elements of the story, including the conjuring of the dwarf-cashew grove and the appearance of the lost and injured merboy, force her to confront this desire to escape the past. The sight of the dwarf-cashew grove, the grove's gate, and the feel of the cashew fruit in her hand flood Calamity with memories of her childhood. Her mother had carefully tended to the cashew grove, while her father let it become a tangled mess of neglect and rot after her mother's disappearance. Although she first describes the grove as bountiful and reaching joyfully toward the sun, darkness begins to creep into her description as Calamity realizes that "something else must have been nourishing [the trees] down below the waters." Soon the experience becomes overwhelming to her senses. "The smell. I had forgotten it; the cloying sweet smell of hundreds of fallen cashew apples. The reason I hated cashew juice, though I could drink distilled cashew liquor; the smell of the alcohol was quite different than the smell of the fruit. And now I was mashing overripe cashews beneath my feet with every step, releasing that overpowering odour into the air" (Hopkinson, *New Moon* 169). Calamity's olfactory overload mirrors the intensification of terror as she moves deeper into the grove. The branches lace together like threatening fingers, the darkness deepens, and Calamity begins to catch moving shadows out of the corner of her eye, wondering about potential evil spirits or jumbies that may be closing in. Scared by arms closing around her, she turns in fighting stance only to discover that Gene, her love interest, had arrived and walked into the grove to find her. Distracted by physical affection as she often is, she dismisses the appearance of the dwarf-cashew grove and allows herself to be swept up in the drama of a new affair.

Calamity's horror in Hopkinson's novel is not only tied to a fear of the supernatural unknown, but also deeply tied to a fear that repressed memories and stories from her past kept from her by her parents might reemerge. Had her father killed her mother, as the community had long speculated? Had her mother simply disappeared into the night, frustrated by the weight of motherhood and marriage? Or had her mother found her stolen monk-seal skin and returned to the ocean to live again as a merperson? This potential legacy feels lost to time as the only two people who might have answered those questions are gone. From this loss, the manifestation of rememory springs, bringing with it horror and, ultimately, healing of these familial relationships.

Just as the recovery of memory in *The Good House* allows the protagonists to identify threats to the community, Nalo Hopkinson's *The New Moon's Arms* marries the repair of cultural and familial memory not only with improved interpersonal relationships but with larger structural threats to the community. The surrounding waters of her fictional island are filled with monk seals, which, folklore holds, are the animal descendants of enslaved Africans who walked into the sea to become seals rather than capitulate to slavery.

However, these stories are appropriated and whitewashed, using thin, blond, white mermaids with "tea-cup breasts" to advertise to tourism, erasing the presence of the Black merpeople, and the history of trans-Atlantic slavery that brought them into existence. As Anatol notes, "Hopkinson asserts the creation of a new people and a new culture in a new environment: literally, the seal-people, but symbolically, the generations born out of the trauma of slavery, the spiritual power of a captured people, and the need to adapt to new places and spaces" (Anatol 208). The erasure of the Black merpeople and their replacement with models of white femininity enacts a symbolic violence against the Black community of the island. This "new world" creation finds itself threatened again not just by symbolic erasure, but by the poisoning of the waters by a large salt company dumping runoff into the waters. The recovery of Calamity's own memory allows her to recover cultural memory of the creation of the merpeople and the dada-hair lady and draws her attention to the environmental threat.

In each of these novels, memory becomes an instructive device for identifying threats to the community, discerning positive and negative intentions, and providing ideas for how one might approach these threats. For instance, in *The New Moon's Arms*, Calamity's homophobia and obsession with her daughter's appearance harms the relationships she would have with both her daughter and her daughter's father. Because each interaction is halted at this level of engagement, it also blocks Calamity from joining in the protest actions in which Ifeoma, her daughter, and Ifeoma's father, Michael, are involved—specifically, aiding in the fight to save the destruction of the environment by the salt corporation that is illegally dumping chemicals into the waters surrounding the factory, which subsequently endangers the sea people. Connecting with her past trauma and ancestral trauma allows her to understand how white mainstream culture normalizes the mutilation of difference (the merchild undergoing surgery to "fix" his knees), the emotional exile of LGBTQ+ folks from Black communities, and her internalized slut-shaming.

CHAPTER 2

Memory, Decolonization, and Alien Invasion in Nnedi Okorafor's *Lagoon*

A continuing criticism of science fiction, as recently as 2019, among the general populace and specifically Black audiences is that, in the face of real-world issues like water wars, famine, the use of child soldiers, or the plight of refugees, the genre is irrelevant. After all, what good is imagining spaceships and aliens when reality is unsettled and nonfictional people are in danger? Although these critics often prefer stories that offer more realistic explorations of these critical issues and their effects, African realist literature and science fiction, the latter of which Walidah Imarisha and adrienne maree brown refer to as "visionary fiction," have much in common. George Joseph notes that "African writers, taking their cue from oral literature, use beauty to help communicate important truths and information to society. Indeed, an object is considered beautiful because of the truths it reveals and the communities it helps to build" ("African Literature" 351). The same is true of Afrofuturist and Africanfuturist science fiction. As a problem-solving genre, it is considered most successful when it imagines possible future worlds, problems we might face, and how we might address them, revealing important truths and shaping communities of fans, and increasingly, activists.

Among science fiction scholars, the genre has long been understood as one through which contemporary social issues are explored, shifting our frame of reference to interpret these problems in new ways. John Rieder's book *Colonialism and the Emergence of Science Fiction* traces the genre back to the Western world's fascination with exploration and the untapped riches of "the lost races." This connection with the history of colonialism forms part of the general dismissal of the genre, fueling the continuing belief among many fans that only white Western writers produce stories using the tropes of science fiction and fantasy and any attempt to acknowledge racial or other difference in science fiction is simply an example of twenty-first century "woke politics."

However, science fiction is certainly not limited to the Western world and indeed existed by another name well before the emergence of the genre alongside colonialism. Despite the explosion of literary and filmic science fiction from across the African continent in the last ten years, science fiction and fantasy have been present in various African cultures well before their official inclusion within the genre. As Kenyan science fiction film director and author Wanuri Kahiu argues, science fiction and fantasy are not new genres in African forms of literature and storytelling. Beings from space, seers, talking animals, and sentient plants have appeared in stories communicating morality and tradition, as well as societal codes of conduct and behavioral mores, across the African continent (Kahiu). Kahiu's comments form part of a growing movement of African science fiction writers who are expanding the definition of science fiction beyond a solely Western and predominately white genre. Nnedi Okorafor distinguishes this movement as Africanfuturism, highlighting the centrality of cultures from the African continent in their artwork (Okorafor, "Africanfuturism"). Their artistic voices redefine existing African writing and storytelling practices, as well as contribute to the larger science fiction canon. In addition, these writers explore the legacy of colonialism and use the tropes of science fiction to work toward decolonization of African cultures. As Ivor Hartmann, editor of the collection *AfroSF*, maintains, science fiction "is the only genre that enables African writers to envision a future from *our* African perspective" (Hartmann 7). Indeed, Joshua Yu Burnett notes the existing tropes and traditions in African literatures that allow for a reading that would situate them with the science fiction canon. Burnett remarks upon the symbolic violence that occurs when we refuse to recognize the contributions of Africans to our shared imagined futures (Burnett 121). Both Hartmann's and Kahiu's remarks emphasize that writing from an African perspective is already embedded with science fiction and fantasy tropes. Equally revealed in each is the importance of cultural memory in this envisioning of a future uncoupled from colonialist narratives.

The most well-known author writing with the purpose of remembering traditional African culture while examining the future is Nigerian-American Nnedi Okorafor. Her 2014 novel *Lagoon* tells the story of a Nigerian marine biologist, a Nigerian soldier, and a Ghanaian rock star at the moment of an alien invasion. Upon the aliens' arrival in Lagos, Nigeria, the three are drawn together to introduce the aliens to the rest of the human world. Toppling multiple social hierarchies and cleansing the oceans, these shape-shifting aliens who proclaim themselves to be catalysts of change inspire nationalist pride and expel the lasting influences of colonialist rule. Among her motivations to write *Lagoon,* Okorafor cites a particular "strain" of evangelical Christianity at work in Nigeria. Naming religious figure Bishop Oyedepo of the Living Faith Church Worldwide, Okorafor calls attention to the denomination's history of violence against women, particularly those deemed "witches" who are slapped across the face in the name of the Lord. In a blog post about the novel, Okorafor writes, "What worries me about the particular strain that's been running through Nigeria in recent years . . . is that it's teaching Nigerians to hate their own indigenous traditions, spiritualities, and religions. It's one thing to move past what was there before. . . . It's another thing entirely to move past what was before because of a nasty form of hatred of one's self in the guise of religion, brought or imported by outsiders and foisted upon people" (Okorafor, "Insight"). While others have examined the ecofeminist implications of the novel as an example of Oceanic Afrofuturism in the genre of petrofiction (Jue), this chapter examines how Okorafor activates local and cultural memory via science fiction tropes to push back against the ideological tide of this strain of Christianity and imagine a world where Nigerians might not only reject the self-hatred embedded in these teachings, but embrace a larger decolonization that discards Western cultural imperialism.

Unlike American science fiction of the Golden Age that employs alien invasion to explore anxieties about the threat of domination by a foreign "Other," Okorafor envisions a peaceful first contact that decenters the West from narratives of intergalactic importance. The novel does not suggest Nigeria as a new site of international focus that uncritically accepts the history of colonialism, simply elevating Lagos to the perceived prestige of New York City or London. Okorafor posits a new invasion of Nigeria that expels the exploitation of the Western world. Christian missionaries lose control of their congregations, and the power of the old gods is returned. The ocean waters off the coast, once polluted and deadly, are cleansed, restoring marine health. Framed as an "awakening," Okorafor's contemporary alien "invasion" reconnects Nigerians with precolonial cultures and strengthens Africans' own personal and political power.

While the nations of Africa have reached a formal end to the period of colonial holding, colonial intervention continues through a rhizome of multinational corporations that draw on the continent's natural resources, Christian missionaries who espouse and preach Eurocentric worldviews, and nongovernmental organizations that frame Africa as in perpetual need of aid and Western intervention. Gayatri Spivak has referred to this mesh of ideological and physical influences as the postcolonial neocolonized world. Decolonization asks how we can end neocolonialism, which contains elements of political, economic, and underlying ideological influences of the Western world. What Ngũgĩ wa Thiong'o refers to as the "cultural bomb," or cultural imperialism, perpetuates the anti-Blackness and anti-Africanness that undergirded both the transatlantic slave trade and the colonization of Africa by European powers. In addition to the forces of imperialism that promulgate this anti-Blackness, Ngũgĩ notes there exists an opposing force at work in Africa today: the tradition of resistance (Ngũgĩ). Drawing attention to the ideological strength of the imperialist tradition, he suggests the role of intellectuals must be interrogated, pointing out how African intellectuals have been complicit in propagating this cultural imperialism by adopting European languages for academic work and excluding those who write in indigenous languages, using English mastery as a gatekeeping mechanism, and blocking access to sites of knowledge production. These mechanisms that discourage the use of indigenous language or the study of African culture have the knock-on effect of subtly, and sometimes not-so-subtly, disassociating these cultures and forms of cultural memory with notions of knowledge production and/or progress. After all, Frantz Fanon argues that "to speak means being able to use a certain syntax and possessing the morphology of such and such a language, but means above all assuming a culture and bearing the weight of a civilization" (1). The process of decolonization also involves taking intellectuals to task and placing "African discourses at the center of scholarship on Africa" (Creary 2). Equally important, however, is the need to escape a system where humanity is divided up along a human-inhuman binary based on white supremacist discourse.

Similar to critiques of African American respectability discourses that claim a "proper" performance of humanity will ensure the accordance of the same level of human rights accorded to whites, or of Booker T. Washington's insistence on racial uplift through economic development, Creary notes that "Africa cannot escape its subjugation within modernity by simply by attempting to climb up through 'development,' as development does not disperse the anti-blackness and the anti-Africanness of Western modernity" (Creary 2). He suggests that equality is also accessible through the creation of a new system of social organization. Valuing cultural memory and what makes ethnic cultures of Africa unique must also form part of this escape from subjugation.

Decolonization is marked both by the desire for reclamation of a precolonial era as well as the revitalization or recognition of an ongoing resistance. The fusion of past, present, and future equally serves as a central aspect of Afrofuturism's attempt to project a Black future while addressing the social ills of the present. This synthesis is revealed in Okorafor's novel where alien invasion acts as the force by which a new social organization is both revealed and remembered. In addition to using alien "invasion" as a trope to expose the intricacies of the fight between the imperialist forces and forces of resistance that exist in Africa, Okorafor equally highlights the need for a radical intervention to escape Western cultural imperialism. The aliens of *Lagoon* represent an opportunity to escape the anti-Blackness and intimate tyranny of the postcolony. Their arrival introduces of a mode of thinking about life that draws on existing African mythologies and religions, but is wholly loyal to no group, Western or African, and dismantles the harmful practices and ideologies of each while allowing the most life- and spirit-affirming and sustainable qualities to surface. Memory functions in the novel to imagine a future with room for African traditions and cultures that does not reify Western modernity alone.

Neocolonialism in *Lagoon*

Father Oke is a major vector by which neocolonialist ideology is represented in the novel. As a Christian fundamentalist leader who espouses the prosperity gospel, Oke draws on the faith of his worshippers to build his own earthly wealth, demonstrated by his expensive suits, perfectly maintained luxury cars, and palatial residential compound. The pageantry of Oke's position and his insistence on using the patriarchal title "Father" represent what Achille Mbembe refers to as a "desire to shine," or a representation of the intimate tyranny that marks the internalization of an authoritarian epistemology (66).

This fictional representation of Bishop Oyedepo is a deeply misogynist character who espouses an anti-Black, anti-African worldview expressed plainly in his interactions with his parishioners: "He had to work hard to keep his disgust from showing. He could almost smell her. Peasant, he thought. Rubbish. Filth. But he would take her money" (Okorafor, *Lagoon* 52). Revealing Okorafor's concern that this type of fundamentalist Christian ideology teaches Nigerians to "hate their own indigenous traditions, spiritualities, and religions," Oke rejects attempts by parishioners to blend their indigenous beliefs with Christian dogma. As a woman steps forward to claim "I am a winch. I am not a winch, but a winch for Jesus," Father Oke flies into a rage and slaps her to the cheers of his parishioners (Okorafor, *Lagoon* 53). The initial disgust Oke expresses about this woman—emerging both from his misogyny and internalized racism—accretes around the ways she has failed to adopt white Western appearance and cultural markers. His negative remarks focus on how she has failed to chemically process her hair and "improperly" refers to herself as a 'winch' rather than a 'witch,' revealing the depth to which English functions as a gatekeeping mechanism of neocolonial control in the novel. Finally, the very act of claiming "witch" status, even as she claims a power to effect change which she chooses to employ "for Jesus," suggests that the woman is not fully deferential, accepting her subservient role.

It is important to pause and note the specificities of witchcraft in African cultures. While both men and women might be witches, there is a gendered component to the stigma attached to witchcraft that disproportionately finds women accused of witchcraft. Men accused of witchcraft are not as stigmatized as women and, in cases where these men are seen as powerful political leaders, the witchcraft that is attributed to their success might be celebrated as a form of power that can ward off the attacks of other powerful forces, particularly when those dangers originate outside the community (Austen 91).

Okorafor's unnamed female parishioner, who openly claims to be a witch while pledging loyalty to Jesus, appears to be attempting to model herself after these powerful male witches whose power might protect the community from invading forces. However, her gender and inability to reproduce English to the standard set by Father Oke mark her as an unacceptable aberration that must be shamed into submission. In the act of slapping her, Oke acts not only as a force for neocolonialist thought, but also as a voice that impedes the development of a unifying nationalist identity that might serve to block forces of literal or cultural invasion.

Father Oke's intervention in Adaora's marriage represents another example of neocolonial misogynoir. One of the novel's three protagonists, Adaora, the marine biologist, is among the first to be contacted by the aliens and is tasked with introducing them to the world. Drawn to Bar Beach after a physical altercation with her husband, the first in her marriage, which she characterizes as previously having been loving and supportive, Adaora reflects on her relationship, recounting the fight in which he refused to allow her to go to a concert and then beat her when she dared to question him. Although Adaora does not hold Father Oke completely at fault, citing the more subtle influences of Chris's interfering mother and the stresses of his high-profile job, she notes that the marked change in his behavior and beliefs began once he started attending Father Oke's church. The home laboratory he had once happily provided for her in support of her work as a marine biologist, he now refers to as a "witch's den." As his beliefs shifted, Adaora's scholastic achievement had become not a marker of her success and a source of familial pride, but rather an indicator of Adaora's aberrant gendered behavior as "a marine witch," able to control water and all its force. When confronted with the alien, Ayodele's shape-shifting ability, her husband makes these suspicions clear:

> "You've poisoned me! Witch! I knew it! I am hallucinating because you've poisoned my body, o!" He took more steps back. "I shower my wife with everything she wants, only to realize I've fed the devil!" He stumbled toward the stairs. "Marine witch, o!" he wailed, pointing at her. "*Amusu*! I knew it! I knew it! Jesus Christ will send you back to hell, o! God will punish you! In the name of Jesus and the Holy Spirit." (Okorafor, *Lagoon* 25)

After this confrontation with his wife, a deeply distressed Chris turns to Father Oke for guidance. Again, Oke reveals the depths of his misogyny as grounded in biblical thought: "Women are . . . weak vessels. It is identified in the Bible. Your Adaora is a highly educated biologist but she's no different from the others. She could not change herself if she tried" (Okorafor, *Lagoon* 29). Although Chris begins to express doubt that his wife is indeed a marine witch, Father Oke reaffirms his suspicions, citing Adaora's understanding and knowledge of water as evidence of her witchcraft.

In addition to Father Oke's support of domestic violence, he counsels Adaora to make peace with her husband despite the beating he had recently delivered. Enraged, she asks Father Oke,

> "And how can we make peace when you are constantly meddling? You instruct him to starve himself like someone who does not have food! You convince him of your twisted nonsense." She stepped closer and Father Oke stepped back. "How does him *slapping* me in the *face* bring peace, *Father*? Eh? How can a man slap his wife 'in the name of Jesus?' *You* instructed him to do so! You think I didn't see your email to him a week ago? 'Break her with your hands, then soften her with flowers.'" (Okorafor, *Lagoon* 38)

These interactions between Chris, Ayaode, and Father Oke make clear the misogynist rule of evangelist Christianity, but also Oke's employment of witchcraft as an accusation against Ayaode draws on anti-Africanness in his rejection of even the suggestion of African traditional religion.

Only two characters in the story touch all other characters, large and small: Father Oke and Ayodele, the alien ambassador. Whether they respect or despise him, Oke's impact on all of the characters, as either a pastor, "smooth-talking predator" (37), or fellow con man, represents how neocolonialism operates, introducing self-doubt and self-hatred into the minds and hearts of all Nigerians. Love him or hate him, each character must react to him. His is the ideology to which all respond in some way and cannot simply escape or ignore. This relationship to neocolonial ideology is what Mbembe refers to an "intimate tyranny," in which "the practices of ordinary citizens cannot always be read in terms of 'opposition to the state,' 'deconstructing power,' and 'disengagement'" (128). Whether one performs rituals of deference, such as the parishioners who gather for sermons and seek guidance, or participates in performances invoking laughter at the state, both actions reinforce the notion that their power is unquestionable. So, too, have each of the characters absorbed some level of anti-Blackness and neocolonial ideology.

Decentering Western Cultural Imperialism

The spread of the aliens' influence labeled the "Awakening" marks the end of Western cultural imperialism in the country as indigenous cultures and the "tradition of resistance" gain power in the novel. Ayodele uses telepathic ability to seize control of Nigeria's telecommunications networks and announce the aliens' arrival while the aliens leave ship in larger numbers, shifting the cultural landscape immediately. Recognizing the conflict with Christian dogma that posits human life as the center of the universe created by the arrival of the alien ship and the potential loss of faith and concurrent loss of his power, Father Oke plans to convert Ayodele and thereby affirm the would-be literal, universal power of Christianity, and strengthen his own position of power and fame. Forming a mob outside Adaora's home, Father Oke calls on the power of the Bible as the word of God and whips his parishioners into a violent frenzy, throwing bricks and Molotov cocktails into the home when not allowed to speak with Ayodele. Alien ambassador, Ayodele, seeing the hypocrisy of their violence, refuses be swayed to work for the forces of Christian indoctrination. This humiliating and public failure of Oke's attempt to convert and co-opt her power results in the loss of his flock who abandon him shortly thereafter.

Another marked cultural shift occurs with the arrival of the aliens, eschewing the Western worldview in which humans sit at the top of a global hierarchical order, dominating all other forms of life—a worldview critiqued by Donna Haraway among other ecofeminists—occurs early in the novel. Humans are not the first residents of Earth to interact with the aliens; instead, the reader experiences their arrival via the perspective of a swordfish, drawn to the "sweet" pure water the alien vessel was creating. As the swordfish swims closer, he finds himself among a "welcome delegation" of diverse marine life greeting the aliens, attracted by the clean water, light, and sound. While Western readers may view the importance of marine life as the "welcoming committee" as a disruptive force, this remains a mode through which Nigerian culture is transmitted. Animals hold a place of extreme importance in African storytelling and mythology where creatures might be seen as messengers of gods or as living incarnations of deities (Beecham 176).

As Melody Jue argues, the novel "constitutes a practice of resistance against western paradigms of scientific practice that are centered around the control and domination of nature based on gendered forms of 'knowing' carnally and cognitively" (174). This form of knowledge production, predicated on human superiority, is disrupted by Okorafor's use of the perspective of the animals to highlight how life is connected on the planet, forming an intricate ecosystem in which all entities and structures influence each other. In addition, this choice moves us away from the human-inhuman binary which reproduces anti-Blackness and anti-Africanness, providing the systemic change for which McCreary called.

The author's extradiegetic dedication reinforces Okorafor's interest in disrupting the distinction: "To the diverse and dynamic people of Lagos, Nigeria—animals, plant, and spirit" (Okorafor, *Lagoon* 18). This dedication is reflective of the beliefs of the Ashanti, the Igbo, and the Yoruba, who each hold that "everything in nature, including plants, animals, and inanimate objects, is believed to have a spirit or soul or governing principle and a function in addition to a certain level of spiritual power" (Hazzard-Donald 24). Each of these ethnic groups, each present in Nigeria, recognize the connection between humans, animals, and plants, recognizing them as dynamic agents. These marine animals play the role of ambassador to alien life that ultimately unsettles the forces of cultural imperialism among the people of Lagos, representing the "Awakening" of the forces of resistance and contributing to the resurgence of cultural memory.

Ijele, the Importance of the Masquerade, and Cultures of Resistance

As the process of "Awakening" continues, multiple battles for the hearts and minds of the citizens of Lagos play out. Ainehi Edoro's review of *Lagoon* applauds Okorafor's realistic portrayal of Lagos: "There is the Lagos of everyday life—traffic gridlock, internet cafes, 419ers, questionable pastors, hustling university students, African Hip-hop, underground LGBT groups, and beach nightlife. This Lagos is portrayed in all its chaotic allure" (Edoro). From this mélange of people and cross purposes, the 419ers and the internet cafes from which they operate form a significant nexus through which we see Nigeria's culture of resistance and how the alien intervention catalyzes that resistance into a more effective form of decolonization.

"419" is the Nigerian term for specific types of internet fraud, such as the "Nigerian Prince" scam in which people are asked to wire funds to a temporarily financially embarrassed Nigerian prince who will return the loan many times over once the crisis has passed. *Lagoon* introduces us to a group of 419ers, with a particular focus on one who gives himself the code name "Legba," a play on the name of the Yoruban trickster god of language, communication, and the keeper of the crossroads. Borrowing the name and the function of the trickster, this young man is not what he claims to be and, just as the trickster turns the tables, using his wit to outsmart a seemingly stronger opponent, the 419er Legba uses his enemies' weaknesses against them—in this case, white Americans' ignorance of and assumptions about Nigeria and Africa in general. Positioning himself as a righteous criminal, Legba notes,

> My plan was genius. Seriously, the woman was an idiot. She really believed her Caucasian blood and money made her irresistible to one of Nollywood's top film directors. She'd even told me these things in those exact words. She had no clue that she sounded like a racist condescending asshole. There was a very pure strain of White Privilege running through her. So why not capitalize on her idiocy? (Okorafor, *Lagoon* 189).

Using this scam, 419ers turn Americans' and Europeans' ignorance of Africa in general, stereotypes about the poverty and primitivism of Nigeria despite the country's relative wealth, and racism against people of color and Africans in particular, against them. In this way, 419ers use a common tactic among con artists of all stripes, in which they entice a "mark" into feeling as though he or she is the one taking advantage of the naïve in order to use the mark's greed against them. However, in turning not just greed, but racism and ignorance against white people, Okorafor reveals both the idiosyncrasy of Nigerian con artists and the culture of resistance that exists before the arrival of the aliens.

Although we might read Legba's scam as a form of resistance, it is one that depends on ignorance and racism while doing nothing to challenge it directly. One might imagine that by playing into the mark's assumptions, he is reinforcing suspicions about the untrustworthiness of Black people. While it certainly works to line the pockets of the scammer, it does little to nothing to challenge the larger systemic issues of racism, calling into question the efficacy of this approach to resistance. Indeed, the arrival of the aliens brings about a dramatic change of heart for Legba.

On the day of the "Awakening," while working the 419 scam even in the midst of the city's destruction, a masquerade of the African deity, Ijele, known as the "chief of all masquerades," representing Igbo royalty, comes to life. The Ijele masquerade, typically a full-body mask representing the deity that a select festival goer might don, appears not as the man-made structure imbued with life by the wearer, but alive in its own right. Taller than the internet café building had previously been before falling to rubble around Legba, Ijele floats above the ground, unbothered by the debris at his feet standing over thirty feet high. The masquerade's wooden structure is covered with bamboo sticks, canes, and ceremonial cloth decorated with colorful geometric patterns and shifting designs indicating that the masquerade is actually alive. Each of the tiers feature small human figurines, each scurrying across the tiers while a giant yellow serpent, the "sign of Igbo pride and mightiness," sits coiled and gazing at the situation below (Okorafor, *Lagoon* 191–92). Legba, astonished, describes the music emanating from the living masquerade as "impossible" and "the sound of life, the beginning" (Okorafor, *Lagoon* 192).

Okorafor's use of the masquerade, a ritual in which a costumed performer pays homage to ancestors and spirits in addition to soothing community tensions among the living, is a powerful example of how the aliens do not simply remove the effects of Western cultural imperialism, but also provide an opportunity to address aspects of social injustice that exist in both Western and African cultures. Attending first to the decolonization and reification of indigenous culture in the passage, within various African cultures, masquerade exists within a tradition of resistance, similar to Bahktin's reading of the function of carnival as a transgressive ritual with the power to make structural changes. However, it equally operates as a "principal presence in the restoration of social balance in traditional Igbo societies" (Ezeliora 46).

Indeed, the masquerade in Igbo culture serves multiple cultural purposes, one of which is the reinforcement of social norms and "the masquerade as spirits of the dead—'Mmonwu,' 'Mmanwu' or 'Mmuo,' in Igbo culture area; 'Egungun' in Yoruba land, 'Egwu' or 'Eguata' in Igala area, 'Alekwu' in Idoma, 'Ekpo' in Efik, and 'Ekpe' in Ibibio, portray its widespread ideology of spiritualism" (Ugwu 20). As Ugwu notes, the masquerade inspires both awe and loyalty in the participants and witnesses, and this is equally demonstrated in the interaction between Ijele and Legba. It is no coincidence that the masquerade came to challenge Legba's criminal behavior, as some Igbo masquerade rituals are vectors for expressing ethical ideologies, addressing antisocial behavior by calling forward those who have violated norms in front of the larger community. One example is the celebration of a "night spirit called 'Ayaka,' 'Ajukwu' '(Achukwu),' 'Onyekulum (Onyekurunye)' or 'Osulugwogwo'" who represents a means of enacting justice and restoring those who deviate from social norms to the communal fold. Parading around the peripheries of homes, these masquerades sing songs satirizing community members, ridiculing them with derogatory names, and exposing community members' criminal deeds, warning them to repent (Ugwu 21). Moving from home to home in this way, members of the ethnic group call out people who exhibit antisocial behaviors violating the norms of communalist society. Ijele, along with one of the aliens, destroys the internet café, demonstrating the "invasion's" dramatic ability to unseat Western discourses by strengthening the existing power of resistance.

An additional dimension to this unseating is the instillation of nationalist pride rooted in Afrocentric identity in the 419 scammer. Feeling a rush of Igbo pride at the "miracle" witnessed, Legba has a realization that his days of fraud are over.

> This was something I could tell my grandchildren about, if I lived. I was witnessing a miracle. My days of fraud . . . even as I knelt there under the table, I knew they were over. It all became clear to me in that moment. All that had been happening for the last several hours. The terrorist [Ayodele] who'd hijacked all the computers and mobile phones. We'd all watched her speak, but still we were focused on our own things, on getting what we could get. I was so focused on getting the white woman to pay, even when the madness washed into the streets. But this woke me up. The coming of Ijele. I am not being melodramatic and I am not crazy. And I am not out of danger. But I will never practice fraud again. Never. I swear. As I cowered under that table and watched Ijele and the man whom I now believed was one of the aliens look at each other, I felt this great swell of pride and love

for Nigeria. I felt patriotism. I would die for it. I would live for it. I would create for it. This was real. Tears were streaming down my face. (193)

As Papa Legba, the keeper of the crossroads, the spirit who guards access to all other deities, we might interpret that the scammer himself is at a moment of personal crossroads in which he might continue to overinvest in others' definitions of his culture or he might begin to appreciate and develop a sense of pride of Nigerian culture. This, too, falls within the realm of uses of the masquerade. As Ugwu proposes, masquerade might well be used as a means to create a nationalist identity for Nigerians, addressing the problems of nation, uniting disparate ethnic groups with folk theatre traditions and ideologies (19). "In order to emulate these qualities for purposes of national development, Nigeria becomes envisioned as a 'major masquerade,' more divine than all the masquerades in her soil put together. Nigeria remains a general religion to all Nigerians and everybody shows sincerity and reverence to her" (Ugwu 28). Whereas political institutions of the nation-state are open to bribery and corruption, Ugwu claims "the masquerades, as spirits, are sincere to the people, they don't accept bribe" (Ugwu 29).

The miracle of the Ijele masquerade coming to life, destroying the means by which the scams are committed, reveals to Legba his own overinvestment in the white world's perception of him and his inevitable failure when playing by the rules or conforming to stereotypes even for the purpose of trickery, calling into the question the limits of this type of agentic behavior. This moment represents an epiphany in which he sees that he must abandon the existing Western ideological system entirely if he is to be truly liberated.

Mami Wata as Challenge to Patriarchal Order

While Okorafor's alien invasion peels back the influence of the Western world, it does not suggest a simplistic return to an unchallenged patriarchal order. For while masquerade reflects ancestor worship and communalist social organization, it also reflects a deep investment in patriarchy. As Ogwu observes in his exploration of masquerade as a traditional theatrical expression of deeply held patriarchal ideologies, only men are allowed to mask themselves and "become" the gods they celebrate. In some masquerades, such as the "Okumpo," men are allowed to have contact with masqueraders and therefore air their grievances, but women are denied this right. In addition, in some village common spaces, elders and prominent male members of the audience are given prime viewing space, while women and children must watch from positions under full sun or other uncomfortable spaces (Ugwu 21). "In many other Igbo settings like Nsukka, Umuoka, Abo, Awka; parts of Imo and Abia states, the patriarchal practice also predisposes the female gender to similar situations, especially where shades and halls are not sufficient for the audiences to sit or stand and watch the play." (Ugwu 21). Through this marginalization, "mystery, fear, and obedience are forced on the women" (Ugwu 7).

Observing performance is just one means by which women are marginalized in the masquerade. Beliefs about women's uncleanliness during menstruation and their inability to keep the spiritual secrets of masquerade block women from becoming initiates, regardless of their age (Ugwu 23). Indeed, this is a theme Okorafor has addressed in previous novels such as *Who Fears Death*, in which the female protagonist, Onyesonwu, fights to participate in the mysteries. Just as Onyesonwu challenges the elders, *Lagoon* remonstrates the patriarchal system within African indigenous religions which have been reinforced by the cultural imperialism of neocolonialism. Okorafor challenges this system through the introduction of the alien, the "tradition of resistance" already present in the protagonist's refusal of her husband's abuse, Father Oke's misogynist fear of witchcraft, and, ultimately, the rise of Mami Wata, the water witch.

Mami Wata appears only briefly in the novel but serves as the vector by which Father Oke rather poetically meets his end. Marking another example of the old gods returning, awakened by the aliens' arrival, Father Oke has already been abandoned by his flock when Mami Wata appears, described as a "mysterious" and "curvy woman wearing tight blue jeans and a white short-sleeve blouse that barely contained her large breasts" approaching him on the beach near the Glass House. Local mythology of the building is that it draws in the Atlantic Ocean, flooding the area because the building is favored by Mami Wata. Amidst the chaos of the alien arrival, Mami Wata observes that "the city is breaking itself, but not one single pane of this building is broken" (*Lagoon* 228). Father Oke's hatred of the building and its ability to withstand the sweeping changes as the aliens unleash the forces of decolonization again marks his misogyny. However, when faced with supreme feminine power in the form of Mami Wata, his perspective shifts as he comes to understand that the woman is indeed a deity, "the goddess of all marine witches." Realizing that he has had contact with both powerful and apparently feminine creatures from outer space and divine beings emerging from African cosmology in "the earth's water" (229) causes him to question why he had slapped his female parishioner and to see both the invisible and entwined hierarchies of patriarchy and neocolonialism: "For the first time in his life, Father Oke truly realized that he lived in a glass palace, while others around lived in a ghetto. He gave up. Father Oke gave in. *What a relief.* They left the Glass House, cross the empty street. They were heading toward the beach. No one ever saw Father Oke again" (229).

While Drewal argues that Mami Wata, frequently depicted as a mermaid, is broadly identified with Europeans in African mythology (197), others such as Krishan regard Mami Wata as a general name referring to the "hybridized river and sea goddesses popularized across Africa and the African diaspora in the nineteenth century" (2). Although popularized during European colonization, the belief in water deities and sacred lakes and rivers predates colonization (Beecham 175). Okorafor uses this "unencumbered spirit of nature detached from any social bonds" as an opportunity to use an existing African symbol as a means of traversing national boundaries and affiliations. This detachment serves to "swallow" Father Oke into the ocean where he is forever severed from his larger community. And while this may seem an antithesis to the masquerade's healing social salve which serves to reconnect members of the community, Father Oke's capitulation to the forces of matriarchal power both signals a sense of personal relief and marks the end of his patriarchal and neocolonial influence among the people of Lagos. It equally serves as poetic revenge for his accusations of witchcraft against both his parishioner and Adaora. This moment provides an interstitial site into which Father Oke can be relegated that indicates the demise of his influence, challenges his religious beliefs, and returns a sense of Africanness to the community. After all, the primary role of Mami Wata is healing or reaching spiritual and material "wholeness."

Mami Wata's connection with Europeans further underscores Father Oke's own association with Eurocentric beliefs and provides a bridge to reconnect him with traditional beliefs. Appearing in a shape and carrying an ideology legible to him as a proponent of the Christian prosperity gospel, Mami Wata functions similarly to Father Oke's brand of Christianity, which suggests faith is rewarded materially. Her arrival in the narrative indicates the beginning of an emotional and mental healing in Father Oke. The relief that Father Oke feels may signal an acceptance of himself and loss of the self-hatred marked by his appropriation of European cultural standards.

Although science fiction traditionally has equated invasion with domination and anxieties about a changing world, the "invasion" of Nigeria in Nnedi Okorafor's *Lagoon* is not about the control of the nation's resources or authority over its people or territory. Okorafor opens the novel with an epigraph from fictional characters who note "Lagos na no man's land. Nobody owns Lagos, na we all get am. Eko oni baje! (Lagos is no man's land.

Nobody owns Lagos, we all own Lagos. Lagos will never be destroyed!)" (Okorafor, *Lagoon* 1). While the arrival of the aliens alters the physical and cultural landscape, these changes re-enliven and strengthen an existing vein of resistance in the cultures of Nigeria. Using the imagery of Ijele, the chief of all masquerades, and Mami Wata, the water deity, as representations of the power of these forces of resistance, likens these forces to sleeping gods. Prodded to consciousness by the shift in perspective brought by the arrival of the aliens, these old gods decenter human supremacy and Western cultural imperialism and a new Nigerian way toward progress is found. This is a world in which benevolent white intervention is neither necessary nor desired. As the presence of their deities suggest, Nigerians' power to affect their own change is already present. Despite this existing power, the aliens equally refuse a simple return to a patriarchal past. Gendered power is challenged throughout the novel, calling attention to domestic violence and women's exclusion from the mysteries. Weaving together these threads of resistance and tradition, the alien invasion is the catalyst for this shift, demonstrating that a radical shift in worldview is necessary to decolonize African minds and recenter African mythologies, traditions, spiritualities, and religions as well as to effect the necessary changes.

Via the science fiction trope of alien invasion, Okorafor, like other science fiction authors, utilizes what Darko Suvin refers to as "cognitive estrangement" to reveal hidden structures of power and loosen their grip on the people. Characters such as Father Oke and Legba reveal the destructiveness of Western neocolonial ideologies not only on Nigeria's economy, political structure, and environmental conditions, but also the caustic effects these ideologies have on the psyche of those who have internalized them.

Okorafor's restorative fabulation employs the tropes of science fiction to restore indigenous beliefs and culture, excising the remnants of colonization and continuing cultural imperialism present in Father Oke's Christianity as well as Legba's capitulation to and reinforcement of anti-African stereotypes as a 419 scammer. The novel explores the emotional weight of that enduring self-hatred, asking readers to recognize the impact it has on them and how it might feel to embrace their culture on its own terms. The revelation of Legba, who comes to love his country and culture as the result of his contact with the Ijele, is a particularly powerful representation of the emotional catharsis the novel invites us to have. As a particularly instructive example of visionary fiction, Okorafor clearly invites readers to critique the role of these messages and how they recreate the anti-Black, anti-African messaging of earlier time periods. Remembrance of these periods and those of precolonial African cultures is the powerful force driving this emotional catharsis.

In this way, the call for remembrance filtered through restorative fabulation with its attendant science fiction tropes of alien contact and "invasion" opens the floor to exploring anti-African sentiment as well as the cultural beauty and power of African cultures, providing an Africanfuturist vision of space in which African nations and their various ethnic groups define themselves for themselves and control their own resources.

CHAPTER 3

Memory and Time Travel in Octavia E. Butler's *Kindred* and Rasheedah Phillips's *Telescoping Effect: Part One*

In our first meeting of the Black Womyn Time Camp 004, Rasheedah Phillips expressed the importance of challenging linear time, noting "many of us don't survive linear time." This comment speaks to the myriad ways in which linear time privileges particular cultural understandings of time and the symbolic and physical violence that befalls those whose cultures do not share Western cultural models. These cultural clashes of temporal models found in what is referred to pejoratively as the "developing world" and in the US among marginalized populations have led to accusations of laziness, an inherently disrespectful nature, disorganization, and a multitude of other sins where temporal discrepancies interfere with the smoothly operating machinations of capitalist growth. In turn, these lead to limited opportunities, the derision of the larger cultures, and the internalization of Western culture as representative of progress and success. We are forced to change or we are left behind. However, stories are where these anomalous temporalities are imagined and preserved. The power of the speculative is the ability to retell and reimagine these cultural models.

Briefly picking up the thread of trauma as it relates to time travel, I am moved by Luckhurst's notion that "no narrative of trauma can be told in a linear way: it has a time signature that must fracture conventional causality" (Luckhurst 9). If Blackness is held "in the wake" as Sharpe suggests it is and should be discussed as being, then we are always experiencing trauma, always experiencing a rupture of linearity and conventional causality (3). This rupture demands we turn our concern toward an understanding of time as not an objective element, but as a socially constructed notion with multiple definitions, limited by the history of Eurocentricity and colonization. Decolonizing time becomes an additional approach to recognizing and healing this trauma. Black women's speculative fiction is one site in which this work of questioning and exploration exists.

Perhaps it comes as no surprise that time travel in Black women's speculative fiction is not driven by the idle curiosity of scientists who wonder at their ability to bend the laws of the universe to their will. Rather, these stories emanate from embodied existence, frequently featuring protagonists who find themselves subject to the whims of the past, imperiled by the past's ability to act upon their person, reaching from the past to the present. In this way, time travel mirrors those realities of systemic oppression that originate in the past and continue to shape the life chances of Black folks in the present. We equally find the protagonist's desire to explore the past converging with the desires of an ancestor to access or shape the future. Unlike the traditional science fiction canon, in the time travel narratives of Black women, human beings of the past are not passive, ignorant beings whose lives are intruded upon by the time traveler. In *Kindred*, for example, the time travel appears to be initiated by Dana's ancestor Rufus as his peril somehow pulls Dana back to the past. Although he may not understand how his power works, he certainly has the desire to use it to shape the future. So too, in *Telescoping Effect: Part One,* does an ancestor understand both the scientific principles of time travel, as well as a desire to cast herself into the future.

The stories I examine in this chapter are grounded both in the trauma of slavery and its successor, Jim Crow segregation in the American South and the de facto segregation operating more informally in the North. Both of these equally draw on Caruth's notion of multigenerational witnessing that suggests trauma cannot be experienced or resolved by the one who lived it but rather is dealt with by others. So, too, does Sharpe suggest contemporary Black folks find ourselves in the wake of a traumatic past. Although rarely discussed alongside memory, time travel is intimately connected with the desire to understand the world beyond living memory, be it a desire to see into the future or to travel to the beginnings of the planet before the evolution of humanity. Where trauma radiates forward in this notion of multigenerational witnessing, Black women's speculative fiction employs the trope of time travel to perform this witnessing, connecting to those ancestors who exist outside of living memory. The resolution of the events in both *Kindred* and *Telescoping Effect* are dependent on intergenerational connections that draw together members of generations separated by time and death in ways that refuse Western models of causality. While the previous chapters examined the loss of cultural and familial memory as a combined source of horror and healing and cultural memory as force for decolonization, this chapter turns to the workings of trauma's nonlinearity, specifically how Black women's memory work in the speculative posits that cultural memory offers a means to effect the decolonization of temporality, opening possibilities for accepting nonlinear understandings of time itself, addressing deeper systemic issues related to anti-Blackness and the association of Western paradigms with logic. In this sense, the interrogation turns away from psychological trauma and healing involved with Black memory in Black women's speculative fiction to turn toward specific concerns of the social construction of temporality and time travel, one of science fiction's core tropes. This chapter examines Butler and Phillips as Black speculative feminist theorists who express a number of concepts useful to reframing temporality in their published works and papers. I also examine Butler's work in the emerging context of sankofarration, which not only looks at how Black authors seek to recover lost histories but also seeks to recover non-Western conceptions of time itself (Jennings cited in Brooks et al. 238).

Western conception of time posits temporality as an arrow, ceaselessly moving from the past to the future, moment by moment. This is far from the only understanding of temporality, however. John Mbiti described traditional African time as a two-dimensional model that constructs time in relationship to community ties. Comprised of the Sasa, the recently deceased who had relationships with living people to remember them, and the Zamani, the deceased with no living person left to remember them directly, this concept privileges the communal and how our understanding of history shifts over time. Rasheedah Phillips, as both an author and activist, explores the Western colonization of concepts of temporality and, like Butler, how family lineage provides pathways for "going back for what was left behind." Drawing together the relationship between memory and an understanding of time as iterative, these works expose the radical possibilities for social organization that emerge via restorative fabulation and the altered perception and definitions of time found in Black women's speculative fiction.

The Importance of Time, Sankofarration, and Black Quantum Futurism

The struggle for self-definition via memory and the notion of temporality itself, or chronopolitics, is at the heart of Afrofuturism's concerns. Often defined as an artistic, social, and intellectual movement that uses the metaphors of science fiction and fantasy and real-world science in its attempts to recover lost histories, Afrofuturism also examines the issues of the present and speculates about possible, likely, and desirable [Black] futures (Phillips, "Future"). Reynaldo Anderson marks science fiction and fantasy as a means to decolonize the Black imagination, while others suggest the refabulation of temporality is an integral part of Black liberation. Multiple Afrofuturist theorists have contributed to the discussion of time, often taking inspiration from the work of Afrofuturist authors, musicians, and visual artists.

Among these theorists is music scholar and author of *Sonic Futures*, Kodwo Eshun. According to Eshun, Black studies has had an understandable preoccupation with the past and the determination to both recover history and to unsettle Western discourses that undermine, discount, or overlook those histories (Eshun). His chronopolitical approach is an extension of this journey to name and claim the past to the political terrain of future spaces. Eshun argues that in addition to considering the past, we must also look ahead and not allow white Western forces to be the only ones contributing to a vision of the future:

> In the colonial era to the middle twentieth century, avant-gardists from Walter Benjamin to Frantz Fanon revolted in the name of the future against a power structure that relied on control and representation of the historical archive. Today, the situation is reversed. The powerful employ futurists and draw power from the futures they endorse, thereby condemning the disempowered to live in the past. The present moment is stretching, slipping for some into yesterday, reaching for others into tomorrow. (Eshun 289)

Afrofuturism is that project that asks us to consider the future in a world that is resistant to Black futures and the people who would articulate them. Eshun notes: "By creating temporal complications and anachronistic episodes that disturb the linear time of progress, these futurisms adjust the temporal logics that condemned blacks to prehistory" (Eshun 297). In other words, we mark ourselves as part of the modern world through a disruption of linear time and thus lay claim to our role in the future.

Graphic novelist and professor of media and cultural studies John Jennings has equally contributed to the notion of time and memory in the literary branch of Afrofuturism by coining the term *sankofarration*, a portmanteau of *sankofa* (a Twi word meaning "it is not taboo to fetch what is at risk of being left behind") and *narration* to define how Black authors employ writing to claim and preserve memory and history. Under the umbrella of Afrofuturism, Jennings's notion of sankofarration further demonstrates that the Western notion of time as solely linear is a cultural construction. "In sankofarration, time is cyclical: "Each moment embodied a recurrence of a past moment, and implied was a potential future recurrence" (Barthold 10).

Equally concerned with the disruption of Eurocentric notions of temporality, Rasheedah Phillips, Afrofuturist author and activist, explores its decolonization in her series Black Quantum Futurism. The first volume, *Black Quantum Futurism: Theory and Practice,* is a collection gathering artists, activist, and scholars to explore the potential of literary and cultural worldbuilding as well as musical and artistic creations as interventions into the "paradigmatically-bound philosophical meta-assumptions" illuminated by Nikitah Okembe-RA Imani (31). Black quantum futurism acts as an umbrella term under which all chronopolitically centered work in the arts, community engagement, and scholarship might be organized. Imani's chapter forms the theoretical contribution at the center of the collection, around which all other artistic and activist interventions orbit. Building on Youngmin Kim's argument about cosmogony as a political philosophy, Imani examines the assumptions built into the very basis of Eurocentric scientific inquiry concerning temporality and the implications of these assumptions, as well as challenges to the Africa-centered scholar seeking to explore and challenge these assumptions. He suggests that "the speculative universe of Eurocentric physicists with respect to time and space possibilities have long been the cultural realities with African traditional societies" (Imani 102).

Theoretical physics has an increasing concern with "metaphysics and ontological and epistemological inquiries that traditionally were the foci of scholars in the social sciences and the humanities" (Imani 35). Using Greenberger and Svozil's article "Quantum Theory Looks at Time Travel" as a case study, Imani considers how the Eurocentric framework of the scholars themselves intervenes in their study at the level of assumption about the "problem" of the logical paradox in meeting one's ancestor or precipitating events that would lead to the death of one's ancestor, as well as their proposed solutions to the issue. Drawing on Mbiti's scholarship on Sasa and Zamani Time as a conception of temporality that is intergenerational and multidirectional, Imani demonstrates that these stand in stark contrast to the Western model of time that moves inexorably and unidirectionally forward. According to this Afrocentric temporal model, one is both connected to the present and to the past of the ancestors and others who shared the geographical and cultural space. The move away from this Swahili temporal model is deeply connected with histories of colonization as African cultures were demonized and Western cultural practices held as markers of progress and "civilized" life. From a Western perspective, futurity came to be conceived in terms of conquest and the development of empire (Phillips, "Future").

The relationship of conquest and empire to notions of progress are equally connected to the development of Western science fiction. John Rieder's *Colonialism and Emergence of Science Fiction* maps the development of various subgenres of science fiction as ideological support for colonialist projects. While imagining the future became synonymous with imagining conquest, early Western science fiction frequently posited lost people or cities of treasure waiting in "unexplored" and isolated locations unknown to white Europeans. This fusion of conquest as progress with the Western temporal model of continuous linear progress into a future time was further cemented in areas of scientific development. For instance, the development of the second law of thermodynamics in the nineteenth century, which suggested that time was continually progressing toward a chaotic universal end, became the only way to understand the universe and the base from which many assumptions about the nature of time and the universe continue to operate (Phillips, "Future"). However, physicists have begun disrupting the solidity of this notion with the study of quantum mechanics and ideas such as retrocausality in which quantum particles in the future move backward through time in order to shape the past. Quantum retrocausality breaks the second law of thermodynamics and operates under a model of time that is both symmetrical and multidirectional, as are the Swahili concepts of Sasa and Zamani time.

Black quantum futurism and sankofarration overlap significantly in their cross-disciplinary pollination and attention to memory and temporality. While science fiction held the power to reinforce notions of time and progress in support of colonial projects of the nineteenth century, Black science fiction, Afrofuturist, and Black speculative feminist thought equally have the power to advocate for additional conceptions of temporality, including those with Afrodiasporic origins. Sankofarration and Black quantum futurism in this context speak to the Afrofuturist writing that that "goes back to collect what might be lost" in the form of a multidirectional challenge to Western temporality. Both of these concepts find expression in the worlds of Octavia E. Butler, who employs terms like "time rogue" and "HistoFuturist" to explain this challenge, as well as the fiction of Rasheedah Phillips, via what she names the Black Grandmother Paradox, a concept standing in opposition to the Grandfather Paradox and causal time loops explored in both Western patriarchal science fiction and quantum theorizing. These concepts expressed in the fictional worlds of Butler and Phillips allow for the retelling of African diasporic time with the potential for decolonizing temporality.

Challenging Western Conceptions of Time in *Kindred*

Among time travel narratives written by Black women, Octavia E. Butler's *Kindred* is the most noted. Butler's 1979 novel features the story of Dana, a young Black woman living in 1976 who is inexplicably pulled through time repeatedly to save the life of her white, slave-owning ancestor Rufus. Multiple scholars have examined the novel's elements of fantasy as neo-slave narrative in the vein of Toni Morrison's *Beloved*, but in recent years, these questions have expanded to include a constellation of scholars examining Butler's theoretical contributions to temporality in her novels and papers. These include interrogations of epigenetics where Dana's story serves as a fantastical representation of the embodiment of the impact of racist environments on Black bodies and its concretized genetic inheritance (Gill 126). Holloway and Setka, on the other hand, examine *Kindred* as Butler's rethinking of temporality and use of Igbo cosmology in the novel. Karla F. C. Holloway notes the fractured and recursive narrative of *Kindred* where Dana moves repeatedly between the past and present as reflective of Dana's spiritual and physical disembodiment and more largely reflective of the notion of ancestry as deployed by Black American writers. "Butler's strategy complicates the perceived distinction between the past and the present until their intersection becomes more real than their separation" (Holloway 113).

This intersection, made tangible in the collision of Dana with her past, demonstrates an understanding of humanity that centers marginalized voices and connects to narratives of Afrodiasporic ancestry, particularly in those locations impacted by chattel slavery. Indeed, *Kindred* forms part of a greater movement of historical fiction and neo-slave narratives that seek to recapture this history in Afrocentric terms. Setka explores the possible metaphors at work, reading the border-crossing Dana as an example of Obganje, a haunting and tormenting spirit who crosses time, as a reflection of Igbo cosmology. Indeed, Butler's papers support this claim and reveal the extent of Butler's interest in Igbo cosmology in research that predates and is coterminous with her completion of *Kindred*.

The necessary, forward-looking chronopolitics for which Kodwo Eshun advocates are evident not only in Butler's published oeuvre, but equally located in her papers where the importance of researching the past and archiving developments of the present in order to extrapolate potential futures feature prominently. Butler's personal practice of "archiving, constellating, and annotating" represents a liberatory fabulation (Streeby 720) that challenges national and institutional memory and "works to expose, and theorize about, the (re)making of time" (Terry 33) as an apparatus for producing counter-historical narratives and forms of radical speculation that provide alternatives to dominant histories and ways of knowing" (Streeby 722).

Butler offers us numerous ways of thinking about time and our relationship to it both culturally and as a species in her notions of "time sculpture," the "time rogue," and the "HistoFuturist." In "Time Sculpture," Butler speculates about what time travel might look like, as an experience of past events outside of oneself, observing with emotional responses diminishing with the repetition of events (OEBP, box 179, OEB 3227). This version of time travel is markedly different from what we are often offered in time travel narratives wherein the time traveler either replaces or displaces themselves, interacting directly with time natives and holding the ability to either change past events or affect future outcomes. Instead, what Butler offers is a mode of time travel that considers the emotional consequences of observing the past, even without the ability to change events. This example of restorative fabulation demonstrates that confronting the past could lead to "insanity . . . [a] permanent retreat into past" (OEBP, box 179, OEB 3227). The lure of seeing loved ones who have passed away or the ability to reexperience moments of great emotional intensity, either elating or devastating, could prove too much and people may be lost to time in ways similar to the repetitive and intrusive thoughts of post-traumatic stress disorder. In this version of time travel, one who could make changes to not only their own lives but others as well would be considered a "rogue, [o]ne to whom time is clay—temporal clay, malleable, how perceived, how manipulated" (OEBP, box 179, OEB 3227). Beyond the scientific wonder of the mastery of time, Butler conceives of the potential devastation of confronting the past, reminding us of the potential consequences therein and the emotional costs to those who engage in looking backward. This is not to suggest that the most emotionally "safe" method is to simply forget the past. Quite the contrary, as previous chapters have demonstrated; forgetting the past, particularly as we remake the world, can have devastating physical, political, and emotional consequences. Restorative fabulation, on the other hand, as a mode of encountering the past, offers the ability to look backward with attention toward one's emotions while doing so, a temporal and historical mode of revolutionary self-care.

As an HistoFuturist, Butler created an archive in order to preserve what might be lost and provided not only the historical record in the form of newspaper articles, books, letters, and ephemera, she also "extrapolate[d] from the human and technological past and present by researching, archiving, and then working over research materials to speculate about possible futures that might materialize on their foundations" (Streeby 721). She saw herself as working along a multidirectional timeline in which a connection to the past, deeply rooted in the understanding of humanity and our motivations and not simply a history of technology or conquest, could provide an understanding of the future and offer the possibility of shaping that future. This notion of archiving is a form of radical reproduction, as Streeby argues, and one that is chronopolitically aware in its preservation of the present and past, is a literal interpretation of memory as theory and memory as liberatory practice. The counter-histories Butler provides in these archives form alternative ways of knowing that firmly place her within the practices Black feminists whose work examine sites outside of the academy for knowledge production (Streeby 722). Indeed, Butler is not only a theorist in this sense, but a literary activist wherein her novels and the speculations found therein are representative of the amalgamation of observations and research borne from the archiving process. Always informed by her archivist eye, her novels and short stories achieve future-casting through Butler's careful attention to contemporary trends and her archiving the evidence of these trends through the preservation of newspaper articles and ephemera. Butler's archival work preserves a snapshot of the social, political, and environmental trends surrounding her oeuvre and provides a set of annotations to her own work, demonstrating an approach to Sharpe's call for new ways of writing and extending the liberatory potential of memory in and around Butler's oeuvre.

Turning toward *Kindred*, time is not unidirectional or linear in the novel. Not only does her ancestor have the ability to pull Dana through time, disrupting temporal directionality, the past occurs concurrently with the present, but moving much more quickly. For instance, when Dana is separated from her husband and travels back to the present without him, he is trapped in the past for years while Dana in the present only experiences a few days. Rather than a linear model, temporality would appear to be coiled where a personal traveling the inner rings would move much more quickly than someone traveling an outer ring of time. When they intersect in those moments, Dana is drawn from her ring to Rufus's ring. Presenting temporality in this fashion challenges the notion of unidirectional, linear time and its associated "disjunction and discontinuity" with an "assertion of circularity, holism, and continuity" (Imani 31) found in Africa-centered conceptions of time and space. As Jennifer Terry notes, the time lapses within the narrative, through which Dana and her husband travel, "open up a sense of plural and non-uniform temporal zones" (Terry 42). The violence of these competing temporal paces is clear in the growing catalog of wounds Dana develops as she called across time and space to save Rufus and facilitate his sexual assault on Alice. While years pass for Rufus, giving him time to heal from injuries and grow, learning the rules of patriarchy and white supremacy, Dana has mere days or weeks between visits during which she is treated to all the everyday cruelties of enslavement, attempted rape, beatings, whippings, and other dehumanizing conduct toward her. The timeline of Rufus's world threatens to keep her from surviving.

Recent science fiction, such as Blake Crouch's novel *Recursion*, explicitly suggests that memory, trauma, and time travel are connected. This is likely due to recent scientific studies examining epigenetic memory and the notion that trauma and other information are encoded in DNA that is then passed on to one's descendants. However, this notion can be found in the speculative literature of Black women and is very much present in *Kindred* well before these specific scientific revelations were widely accepted. Physical trauma written on the body across time appears in numerous instances. In addition to Dana's loss of her arm at the beginning/conclusion of the novel, Rufus's physical peril creates a tension that removes Dana from her own time, pulling her toward him, while Dana's own physical pain and fear of death returns her to her time and restores her self-possession and bodily autonomy. The emotional and physical connections across generations that Butler establishes in *Kindred* are specifically organized around familial connections rather than broad cultural or community connections. Despite Rufus's whiteness having been lost from Dana's family's conscious memory, the DNA they both share cannot be forgotten. The histories of Black and white people in the United States are deeply entangled and cannot be escaped or denied despite the political will of either group to do so. Butler initially offers Rufus up as a child whose view of the world might be altered with Dana's help. However, it is the monstrous power of white privilege and the system of chattel slavery, demonstrated as incredibly seductive, that derails her attempts. Even Kevin, a contemporary man, Dana's husband, despite his horror at the thought of slavery, still finds room for curiosity and wonder at the age in which he finds himself, forgetting the constant danger to his wife in this past world. Between these two white male characters, Butler calls attention to the failures of an approach that emphasizes individual anti-racist intervention. As Butler notes, "I believe that I can bring to writing—to my readers—insight into human relationships. I believe that I can make people see and feel things about their brother and sister humans that they might normally never see or feel" (OEBP, box 80, OEB 1513).

Beyond inviting white readers to empathize, Butler equally asks Black readers to empathize with ancestors. Remembering a particular interaction with a young Black separatist, Butler quotes him saying, "'I wish I could kill off all these old people who've been holding us back, but I can't because I'd have to start with my parents.' Now that man knew the facts of Black history. At the time, he knew them better than I did. But he didn't understand them. He didn't feel them. He professed Black pride, but he was ashamed of his ancestors. They had survived experiences that might have distroyed [sic] him. He had heros [sic] right there in his own family, and he scorned them." (OEBP, box 146, OEB 2927). Storytelling for Butler is a way to alleviate this discontinuity between knowing and understanding. This link between storytelling and memory as a cultural or personal story reveals a key difference between "knowing the facts" and understanding them. In Butler's exploration, memory is a feeling or an understanding, different from "facts." Memory allows for more empathy, fuller understanding of human experiences in the past and the recovery of historical figures as three-dimensional human beings. Indeed, Butler wrote, "The research I did on the Igbo, on colonial New York, on antebellum Louisiana, was all library research. I don't recommend working that way. If I could have traveled at the time, I would have done on-the-spot research as well as the library work." (OEBP, box 146, OEB 2927). While she does not make clear precisely what she means by "on-the-spot research," we may extrapolate from the travels she did to South America to research the appearance of an undeveloped jungle setting and the incorporation of land, plant life, weather patterns, and even the smells of the landscape into the Xenogenesis trilogy that on-the-spot research would involve incorporating the descriptions of visual, aural, and olfactory observations into the story as well in order to contribute to the realism of time travel and the depiction of the three-dimensional humanity of her character/ancestors.

One of Butler's stated goals in her writing is the attempt to spark emotion and create empathy in her readers. Her notes about *Kindred* illuminate these attempts to create empathy in her readers:

Fifty to seventy-five Thousand words
Two to three hundred pages
Very clear   Strong
Intense   Reasonable
   drama,   emotions
MAKE THE READER <u>FEEL WITH.</u> (OEBP, box 80, OEB 1513)

Feeling is central to Butler's notion of time and time travel, especially where time travel serves to connect one with one's ancestors. Not only was feeling and the creation of empathy a motivation behind Butler's desire to write *Kindred*, in order to demonstrate the power and perseverance of ancestors who survived slavery, but feeling and writing holds the powerful ability to transform the author. She noted her resistance in writing the novel *Kindred*: "I didn't want to be come [sic] the main character—time travel as her backward to a backward time" (OEBP, box 146, OEB 2927). Butler feared "becoming" the characters she was writing in *Kindred* through the act of writing itself, channeling their emotions and hers. Butler countered this by becoming a character over which she had more control in *Wild Seed*. "One of the reasons I wrote *Kindred* was to take a look at Black History [sic] in America. I just didn't realize how quickly that history would get personal" (OEBP, box 146, OEB 2927). Butler began writing *Wild Seed* around the same time. This novel features a psychically talented African woman who is coerced into a system of what would become American slavery but refuses to capitulate to that system and ultimately escapes to live her life on her own terms. Butler described this act of researching Igbo ideologies and early American history and writing the novel itself as a balm to the pain of researching and writing *Kindred*.

Seeing writing as an emotional transformation, a becoming, into the character living in the past, the act of writing becomes an emotional time travel. By evoking emotion in her readers, she asks us to time travel as well, becoming her characters. While time travel in *Kindred* as a neo-slave narrative is about the restoration of lost histories, it seems that it is also the restoration of memory and the creation of a cross-temporal connection based on emotion, or restorative fabulation. This act of recovering not just the facts of history but the emotional appreciation for sacrifice and familial pride occurs throughout *Kindred*. Indeed, family and genetics serve as a vector by which the cross-temporal connection can be established in both Butler's and Rasheedah Phillips's work. DNA provides a map that can be used to trace these connections.

Rasheedah Phillips as Activist and Author

Although frequently lauded among Afrofuturists for her activist and organizing work, Rasheedah Phillips is often overlooked as a writer. In addition to her collections on Black quantum futurism, she has produced a collection of short stories and a novella titled *Telescoping Effect: Part One*. While some may find her self-publishing reason enough for exclusion from serious literary analysis or inclusion in the developing Afrofuturist literary canon, her work reflects a guerilla attitude and the grassroots efforts not only of continuing activist work, but also the very roots of Africana Studies and the community work, scholarship, and activism that later came to be institutionalized through its incorporation into academia. *Telescoping Effect: Part One* certainly demonstrates a rejection of literary tropes. As multifaceted as her own blend of archival, activist, and creative work, the novella combines traditional short fiction and graphic novel forms, incorporating newspaper article clippings and a blend of historically accurate and fictional graphs, charts, maps, images, photographs, and quotes, alongside swirling or otherwise distorted text that adds to the emotional impact of the narrative. Extending the narrative beyond the page, Phillips' website, BlackQuantumFuturism.Bandcamp.com, features a soundscape for readers to listen to as they read, creating a fully immersive experience. The extension beyond the page and merging of literary and sonic is not new within Afrofuturist circles. Paul D. Miller, a.k.a. DJ Spooky's *Rhythm Science,* released as a Mediaworks Pamphlet by MIT Press in 2004, equally plays with poetry, theory, and graphic novel visuals, exploring the boundaries of the page as the edge of a record or CD. The pamphlet also contains a sonic and visual component, creating a sonic environment for the consideration of the ideas within the pamphlet's pages.

The ideas of multidirectional temporality, overlooked scientific innovations by Black scientists, and familial relationships as a vector for memory present in Phillip's fiction are supported by and expanded through her edited collections, *Black Quantum Futurism: Theory and Practice, Space Time Collapse I: From the Congo to the Carolinas,* and *Space Time Collapse II: Community Futurisms*. This fertile connection between artists and intellectuals is a clear inheritance of the Black Power and Black Arts movements of the mid-twentieth century. Indeed, we might trace a distinct connection between that thought and its institutional legacy at Temple University, where she studied law.

Telescoping Effect: Part One, published in 2017, jumps between the life of Ma Belle, a retired scientist in 1919, and the then near future life Elaen A'Roz Smith in 2019, a researcher for the Research Coordinates Group (RCG), a company that uses surveillance data from sources as diverse as GPS, police and commercial audio surveillance feeds, satellite cameras, police body cams, and security cameras to shape public perception of past events, or "fixing history." By hijacking the company's technology and the recorded work of her great grandmother, Elaen is able to communicate across time to her ancestor.

Among the many challenges to temporality and memory that Phillips asserts in *Telescoping Effect: Part One* is the notion of memory as an economically exploitable resource. Where African American memory is often overlooked or discounted outside of the bounds of February's month-long call to recognize Black History, Phillips posits a world in which memory becomes a mineable resource and Black bodies and familial connections become a new territory available for plunder and colonization. RCG, the company that manipulates events through the altering of records connected to the events, has extended its reach further, into what Phillips suggests is a form of epigenetic memory. Upon stumbling onto Lula Belle's scientific discovery, the aim of RCG's unnamed "client" seems not to be lauding the contribution of a Black woman to the field of theoretical physics or quantum mechanics, but rather to employ RCG's techniques to manipulate history, manipulate Elaen's own relationship to her family history, and mine Elaen's DNA for access to the past. "Your link to her, to her work, her experiences, is already encoded in you, we are just facilitating the means. Science confirms this. Psychology and social science confirm this" (Phillips, *Telescoping* 32). This reflects the continuing lack of bodily autonomy of Black women in the US, and the ways in which capitalist and white supremacist systems encourage us to devalue and undervalue ourselves to the point that we are willing to sell not just our labor but our cultural memory and genetic heritage in the bargain. Although Elaen wishes to resist this force, she is reminded by her superior that these manipulations will occur with or without her consent. Indeed, Elaen's only opportunity to gain access to the records and technologies of the firm is by collaborating, while secretly working to undermine the operation and manipulate history in her favor.

Highlighting the transmission of racism into new cultural, legal, and technological forms, *Telescoping Effect: Part One* reflects Safiya Umoja Noble's argument that search engines are among one of many ways that ideological bubbles reinforce cultural racism (Noble). These ideological bubbles, exacerbated by social and traditional media platforms, alter perception of recent and past events. The novella reflects this very real cultural anxiety that invites readers to examine the possible economic and political gains of deliberately harnessing the power of media and technology to create, rather than reinforce, ideological bubbles. While making clear the problematic nature of these tools in the hands of a technological corporation that refuses to examine its own racist and sexist practices, Phillips equally explores how these technologies equally offer liberatory potential when freed from those institutions.

Another cultural anxiety depicted in the novella's pages are the rising questions of the limits of a corporation's ownership of an employee's leisure time. As the line between personal time and work time has blurred, we might note the rise of influencers using their lives and bodies to sell products as a deeply blurred space. Social media users find themselves coached to put their best "professional selves" forward in all interactions, and hotbed political issues and political protest can result in penalization by employers. While penalization for participating in protest action is not new for Black protestors in the US, particularly during the civil rights movement of the mid-twentieth century, the rise of social media as a private/public space where many protest actions are organized and shared is specific to our historical moment. As these boundaries between public and private and the employer's time and the employee's time are negotiated, we find ourselves open to the possibility of a new form of corporate ownership of our public selves. Phillips extends this troubling beyond our public selves to our familial selves in ways that mimic the ownership of person and progenitors present in chattel slavery.

Borrowed from psychiatry, the term "telescoping effect" refers to the cognitive temporal displacement of events and is often referred to as cognitive impairment in which one's understanding of linear time is disrupted, casting events long since passed to the present or near past, for example. Phillips's novella imagines the term not as a form of impairment or disorder, but rather as an undiscovered scientific possibility that time might be collapsed in order to achieve contact between the past, present, and the future. The story is told from multiple perspectives, telling the story from viewpoints of Ma Belle and Elaen A'Roz, shifting our timeframe and never centering any one perspective or time period. The familial relationship of the two protagonists is equally important in invoking Africa-Centered Time. Just as Zamani and Sasa time are dependent upon the communal or familial relationship to mark the operation of time, so too does the connection across time and space depend on the relationship of the two women to each other. In this way, time is depicted as fluid and multidirectional, as the reader is drawn from the "present" of 2017 to the past of 1919 and is also sent into the "future" of 2019. We ourselves become a conduit of collapsed time as we read, indicating our own shifting perspective. Time travel by Black women offers the challenge to decolonize our memory, to recognize the inherent power and value in our memory, and equally recognize how to deploy that memory as an oppositional force to white supremacy.

Patricia Hill Collins reminds us how anti-Black cultural interpretations are used to dismiss knowledge production and how, despite clear history of scientific racism, the scientific and technological arenas are often understood as objective spaces devoid from cultural influence. To a certain extent, the scientific method, when followed properly, is intended to minimize this type of interpretative influence. However, we know from history that scientific processes were, and continue to be, abused, with studies conducted in the US used to prove foregone conclusions about the assumed inferiority of Blackness. Because this history concerns the historical development of race in the US or frequently used examples of medical racism and sexism focused on the body, we may forget that this type of cultural assumption equally presents itself at the boundaries of scientific thought, where the imagination of the scientist and the hypothetical converge—for example, when we begin to think of multiverses or nonlinear time. This is not to claim that scientific evidence does not exist in these realms, but rather, the more cutting edge, the less evidence exists, and more imagination is employed to fill the gaps and develop the questions that need to be answered. It is here where we continue to see the evidence of the cultural imaginary and its impact. I believe this is also that space where we can make room for questions stemming from non-Western ideologies concerning the nature of time and the universe. If these are the spaces where "what if" enters the realm of scientific inquiry, then we may look to science fiction and fantasy as rich territories of thought where the African diasporic peoples have imagined how their worldviews shape possible new worlds. The relationship of temporality to memory is one of those locations.

Authors such as Octavia E. Butler and Rasheedah Phillips call attention to traditional African time within the science fiction genre, intervening in the blended leisurely and professional modes of transmission and inspiration that happen between scientists, technologists, and science fiction authors. In an interview for the documentary *Coded Bias*, Shalini Kantayya mentioned the friendship between Arthur C. Clarke and MIT professors, as well as the classes offered at MIT that ask students to design an object or program inspired by their favorite science fiction. This gestures toward the ways in which the arts and sciences communicate between themselves and the importance of amplifying the history and contributions of Black science fiction writers. Black critical imagination has a serious role to play in intervening in these spaces where leisure and profession intermingle. This is part of the chronopolitical call issued by Kodwo Eshun to participate in the creation of the future. Beyond the technology of the everyday discussed in *Coded Bias*, we must also consider the edges of scientific theorizing and the small moments of speculation that exist when confronted with data we cannot yet classify. Enmeshed in a scientific worldview that privileges Eurocentric understandings of temporality, these scientists speculate in ways they may not realize are bounded by these notions of time. The intervention of science fiction by Black women offers a means of introducing worlds in which temporality reflects cultures outside of the white Western paradigm. These selected science fiction novels demonstrate how Black women authoring science fiction have challenged the notion of linear time by drawing on Afrocentric concepts, as well as demonstrate the radical potential of this disruption to intervene in the chronopolitics of the day and accept the invitation to shape our ideal futures.

CHAPTER 4

Memory and the Reproduction of Regime

Anyanwu as *Lieu de Mémoire* in Octavia E. Butler's Patternist Series

Butler's Patternist series, spanning four novels, begins with a dystopian vision of the far-distant future in which humans have developed telepathic powers, organized in a feudal society, and enslaved those without these powers[1]. The telepaths, who call themselves Patternists, find themselves

---

1. The novels were published in an order that, generally, takes us backward through time in the story. For instance, the first novel of the series, *Patternmaster* (1976), takes place in the distant future. The second novel, *Mind of My Mind* (1977), takes place in the contemporary moment, in a world largely similar to that of the United States in the 1970s. The third novel, *Survivor* (1978), is an anomaly in this order and the series at large. This novel follows the story of colonists who have left Earth to escape the Clayark virus that creates the Clayarks we see in *Patternmaster*. The events of the novel take place not only in the distant future, but also on another planet, the only novel in the series to do so. This is also the only novel that Butler refused to reissue and does not appear in the reordered collection of novels issued under the title *Seed to Harvest*. The fourth novel, *Wild Seed* (1980), takes the reader to the origin of the events: the first meeting of Doro and Anyanwu in West Africa. Within the timeline of the series, this is the story that is first in chronological order, although it appeared second to last in the publication timeline. The fifth and final novel in the series, *Clay's Ark* (1984), which tells the origin of the Clayark virus on Earth, takes place in the near future, perhaps a few decades after the events in *Mind of My Mind*. While the books were published out of order, they have since been reissued in a collected anthology titled *Seed to Harvest*. In the anthology, they appear in chronological order, taking the reader forward from the first meeting of Anyanwu and Doro in Africa to the end result of the Patternist world as it wars with the Clayark community.

69

at war with differently evolved humanoids termed "Clayarks." Except for *Clay's Ark* and *Survivor,* the series was written in reverse chronology, revealing the development of the Patternist system and its roots in the trans-Atlantic slave trade. However, Butler's second and fourth novels in the series, *Mind of My Mind* and *Wild Seed,* reveal the role of memory in the liberation of a people. *Mind of My Mind* centers on Mary's orchestrated overthrow of Doro, a being who has spent millennia breeding and feeding on "psychically sensitive" people. Unfortunately, Mary's new system of power replicates its predecessor's more problematic aspects, particularly in the treatment of non-telepathic "mutes." While very few voices in this newly developing community speak out to question this, the most influential of these is an immortal, shape-shifting African woman, Anyanwu, who appears in both novels[2]. Anyanwu's voice acts as a reminder of the cyclical nature of oppression and represents both a connection to the past and the potential for liberation from these structures of domination at a critical moment in the creation of a new governing system.

The role of Anyanwu's memory in this moment of liberation from a colonial regime requires an examination of how we embed memory alongside official histories. Seeing positivist history as static and memory as dynamic, French historian Pierre Nora suggests that the postmodern fracture of unifying history and the tension between the two disparate modes of remembrance has caused a rupture into which we have inserted *lieux de mémoire,* or sites of memory. Museums, memorials, statues, reunions, eulogies, and the like inhabit this space as the "quest of history and the privilege of authenticating memory [has shifted] to everyone" (McKay 262). These *lieux de mémoire* operate outside of the canon of official history and allow a multiplicity of memories and histories to find expression. "Whether deliberately or not, individual or group memory selects certain landmarks of the past—places, artworks, dates; persons, public or private, well known or obscure, real or imagined—and invests them with symbolic and political significance. Thus a *lieu de mémoire* may be a historical or legendary event or figure, a book or an era, a place or an idea" (Fabre and O'Meally 7).

While there is certainly some liberatory potential in the dissolution of overarching narratives, it signals neither the end of official histories nor does it preclude the creation of privileged narrative even within the space of the *lieux de mémoire.* As a function of remembering that is neither wholly official history nor folk memory, *lieux de mémoire* are sites where memory

---

2. The character appears in both novels but has a different name in each. She calls herself Anyanwu (Sun) in *Wild Seed* and Emma (grandmother) in *Mind of My Mind.* I will refer to her exclusively as Anyanwu for clarity.

breaks through official histories, accreting or pooling in the ruptures. We might imagine *lieux de mémoire* as concentrated sites of spontaneous public memory that function quite differently from "history." An official history functions as an accounting of past events that has sedimented into layers of narrative, repeating only the "official" narrative, accruing power to a certain people or nations through this shared narrative and those creators authorized to contribute layers of history, denying the ability to create legitimate narratives to the general populace.

Despite Nora's usage of the term, laden with problematic visions of primitive colonized people, freely living within their precolonized cultures or peasant cultures of Europe's past, memory is a much less rigid account of the past. Memory incorporates legends, folklore, and other forms of storytelling that account for past events in more fluid forms. These were largely overridden in Western cultures via the creation of the official history of the modern age. *Lieux de mémoire*, as a category that exists between these two states, represents a postmodern rupture of the seemingly stable sedimentation of official histories. These forms of remembrance erupt through the layers of calcified history, retaining the spontaneity of memory, open to interpretations and flourishes of storytelling and design to which official histories are not open. Eulogies, for instance, may be spontaneous utterances of grief and remembrance, or they may be curated affairs designed to honor the dead in very specific, forgiving ways. The graveside eulogy might be given only by a wife, while the mistress may not be invited to attend, let alone speak about her relationship with the deceased. Over time, these eulogies, curated and spontaneous alike, may solidify into the official narrative of that person's life.

In *Mind of My Mind*, Butler explores the creation of an official, nationalist, Patternist history at the moment of regime change from Doro to Mary and the potential of Anyanwu as *lieu de mémoire* to disrupt this narrative and re-creation of the problematic aspects of Doro's regime. *Wild Seed*, as the novel in the series that examines Anyanwu's own entanglement within Doro's eugenics, allows us to read the role of Anyanwu as a more powerful player in the creation of Patternist society than she might otherwise be read. While Butler herself refers to Anyanwu as "a quickie character" who would have bored Butler had she been on the scene longer in *Mind of My Mind*, Anyanwu represents a long-standing interest in Igbo culture whose memory holds a potential for righting historical wrongs in *Wild Seed*. Drawing on Nora's notion of *lieux de mémoire*, this chapter examines the role of memory in moments of liberation and the importance of their intervention in the development of new cultural structures and deployment of power in

Butler's novels. Anyanwu serves as a *lieu de mémoire* by defying historical amnesia and acting as a voice of resistance whose memory offers a revolutionary potential as the new regime is born.

Escaping the Regime Only to Rebuild It

Before discussing the Anyanwu's revolutionary potential, we must explore the shift in power from Mary to Doro. *Mind of My Mind,* the second novel in the Patternist series, features the origin of the Pattern, a mental network which connects active telepaths in Butler's series. Doro, an immortal ogbanje figure who takes possession of bodies, prepares to bring two of his active telepaths, Mary and Karl, together in marriage (Butler, *Journal* 1976). Unlike *Patternmaster,* the first novel in the series, which takes place in the distant future, *Mind of My Mind* is set in the 1970s. The story centers largely on Mary, a young Black woman who has yet to transition from latent telepath to active. As Mary is hidden away in a Los Angeles suburb against her will, the reader learns that neither Mary nor Karl have much choice in the arranged marriage and the ensuing procreation that Doro desires, which will happen either via their "assent" or through Doro's possession of their bodies. As Mary reaches her transition, the reader discovers that she is unlike Doro's previous telepaths. Rather than learning to form her own internal shield to block out cognitive and emotional interference of others, she unconsciously reaches out to other active telepaths and connects them all in a telepathic net. This mental snare creates an inescapable pull, drawing each of the telepaths to her physical location to discover what has "leashed" them and, when they realize they cannot free themselves, to find a way to live in this new "pattern" unconsciously established by Mary. Learning to live together and growing in number and ability, power shifts from Doro, as the breeder and master of these disparate telepaths, to Mary, as the leader of a new social order. Unwilling to cede his position of authority to Mary, she is forced to face off against Doro in a life-or-death battle.

Doro's breeding program, already in place for thousands of years when Mary's story begins, invokes the history of eugenics, colonialism, and the trans-Atlantic slave trade. While colonialism is defined by the violent oppression of the Indigenous peoples by an external invading and governing force, it also involves the occupation of land. This aspect of colonization is particularly important in societies where Indigenous peoples understand the land as extension of themselves. Similarly to historic colonialism, Doro's colonization is marked by the violent oppression of the people under his domination via torture, coercion, and reproductive control. While Doro's control of the land of Indigenous peoples is largely invisible in these novels, Doro's possession of the physical bodies of those on whom he feeds is firmly in focus. In this way, alongside the lack of freedom of movement and the control of breeding patterns and labor of his communities, Doro's regime mimics the processes of colonization.

Emerging from Doro's ongoing eugenics program and system of domination is Mary, who figures in the novel as a problematic, postcolonial freedom fighter. Via her arranged marriage to Karl, Doro's strongest active telepath, Mary literally weds imperialism and, ultimately, assumes a place of authority as the result of her formation of the Pattern, a mental network of active telepaths. As the center of the story, Butler asks us to empathize with Mary's neglect as a child, her conflicted feelings of love and hate toward Doro, and the helplessness she feels as she nears transition and is forced to lead a new life with Karl. Doro's conversation about the consequences of injuring anyone, even those who might hurt her, exemplifies this lack of control.

> "What point? That if I'm not a good little girl, [city jail] is where I'll wind up? God! Let's get away from here." Something was wrong with me. Or something was about to be wrong. Really wrong. I was picking up shadows of crazy emotions.
> "Why should we go?" [Doro] asked.
> "My head . . . !" I could feel myself losing control. "Doro please . . ." I screamed. I tried to hang on. Tried to just shut down, the way I had the day before. Freeze. But I was caught in a nightmare. The kind of nightmare where the walls are coming together on you and you can't get out. The kind where you're locked in some dark, narrow place and you can't get out. The kind where you're at a zoo locked up like the animals, *and you can't get out*! (Butler, *Seed to Harvest* 275; ellipses in original)

These vivid depictions of mental interference as Mary nears her transition combined with Doro's ability to physically relocate her and determine her breeding partner against her will demonstrate how little bodily autonomy Mary has. Mary's underdog position of freedom fighter is further strengthened by the history of abuse and the powerlessness that she feels at the beginning of the novel, provoking an empathy in the reader.

Science fiction of the Golden Age positions the protagonist as a champion from humble origins who overthrows an evil dictator to successfully free the people. However, Butler claims these power-seeking political movements may not be as liberatory as they appear and are, in fact, a replication of the very systems they seek to depose. Sandra Y. Govan observes, "Patternists [in *Mind of My Mind* and *Patternmaster*] centuries removed from Anyanwu's village will find themselves repeating this cycle [of] the repetitive brutality of the internal and external slave trade" ("Connections" 84). By positioning Mary in *Mind of My Mind* as a sympathetic figure with good intentions who spawns a highly repressive regime, Butler critiques these political movements, demonstrating the ways in which liberatory efforts and their leaders are susceptible to corruption.

The Pattern that Mary creates, the new structure that promises to free the telepaths from Doro's control, is fraught with contradictions. Although it is initially described as a "leash" for the active telepaths ("actives") trapped in its network, we begin to see the benefits it offers its constituents. The Pattern provides community for the actives, who until its development were painfully isolated and scattered throughout the country. Unable to shield themselves entirely from one another's thoughts, they were intolerant of each other's presence and their telepathic power in isolation afforded them little purpose in their lives. This reflects Doro's stated goal in bringing his telepaths together in order to create a "strong new people" (Butler, *Seed to Harvest* 19). As Butler argues, a lack of purpose results in cruelty and despair as various characters express hateful racism or remain, despite their power, in abusive relationships.

The Pattern transforms these lives, allowing the telepaths to form a community and find emotional stability for the first time. Mary herself begins to feel empathy as she realizes her Pattern can save latent telepaths from a lifetime of misery and mental interference by pushing them toward transition to active status. One telepath's fear of difference seems to dissipate as she finds empowerment in her abilities in psychometry. Another discovers her talents with children and emerges from her shell. The Pattern holds the ability to draw people into a collectivity that inspires loyalty, stability, purpose, and extended kinship networks for its members, affording them a peace of mind hitherto unknown.

However, despite the positive effects this organization has on the lives of the Patternists, there are troubling aspects, not the least of which is the enslavement of the non-telepathic "mutes." The Patternists' emergence from an imperial power structure and the hierarchical organization of the newly formed Pattern taints this attempt at postcolonial freedom. Govan notes the similarities between Mary's Pattern and the kinship networks Anyanwu and, more importantly, Doro used to build power for themselves in *Wild Seed* (Butler, *Seed to Harvest* 84). While both relied on these networks to form a power base, an important distinction should be made between Anyanwu and Doro's acknowledgement of kinship. Where Anyanwu sought to protect as many of her descendants as possible regardless of telepathic ability, Doro relied on difference in the form of psionic ability when acknowledging "family" and therefore those worthy of his interest and protection. This major difference springs from Doro's view of the telepathically inclined as "food" to be consumed when he takes possession of their bodies. Mary is reminded throughout the novel of her similarities to Doro as a "vampire," who takes from unwilling participants through sheer force of power. Mary even appears to desire power similar to Doro's, as evidenced by an utterance made before she transitioned to an active telepath: "Maybe for a change I'd be one of the owners instead of one of the owned" (Butler, *Seed to Harvest* 295). Mary's desire to be an owner rather than owned acknowledges the workings of power within Doro's regime. Noting her own position as one of object rather than subject, Mary expresses feelings of powerlessness in a system that dictates her sexual partnerships. Furthermore, the quote indicates that Mary does not see her transition as a way out of the system, but rather as a shift to a position of power within the same corrupt system. Upon transition she immediately develops "proprietary feelings" about "her people," feelings which Doro himself encourages. Mary's struggle is not truly an attempt at freedom, but rather an inheritance of a deeply flawed system of power.

Although she denies it, Mary is closely related to Doro in design and ambition. As Doro notes, "she's like a scaled-down model of me" (Butler, *Seed to Harvest* 398). While Doro largely overlooks non-telepathic humans, in both *Wild Seed* and *Mind of My Mind*, those under Doro's control rail against his inability to recognize their humanity. In *Wild Seed*, Lale, a highly skilled but brutal sociopath, is allowed to survive, while nonpsychic humans deemed less useful are extinguished. This even extends to those with psychic ability. Doro reveals his plan to breed Anyanwu to the man she has come to see has her stepson, Isaac, and in the following exchange, we can see how Doro sees his project and those he controls:

> "Over the years, I've taken people with so little power they were almost ordinary and bred them together again and again until in their descendants, small abilities grew large, and a man like Isaac could be born."
>
> "And a man like Lale."
>
> "Lale wasn't as bad as he seemed. He handled what ability he had very well. And I've created others of his kind who had more ability and a better temperament."
>
> "Did you create him, then? From what? Mounds of clay?"

"Anyanwu!"

"Isaac tells me the whites believe their god made the first people of clay. You talk as though you think you were that god!" (Butler, *Seed to Harvest* 115)

In this exchange, Doro considers those he breeds to be his "by right" of his power to breed them (Butler, *Seed to Harvest* 252). Seeing himself as godlike in his ability to genetically manipulate humans over time, growing their powers through his breeding program, Doro sees those he manipulates as little more than pawns on a chessboard that only he can see.

The refusal to acknowledge the humanity of those Doro controls is a trait Mary shares. This is particularly evident in the language she and the other Patternists use to describe the treatment of non-telepathic humans. As Mary reflects on the state of the growing Patternist society, she remarks to herself that "they all had to learn to handle mutes—learn not to smash them and not to make robots of them" (Butler, *Seed to Harvest* 419). Mary does not suggest that the Patternists learn not to manipulate the "mutes" or to let them live their lives without the psychic intrusion of the Patternists. Instead, Mary suggests that they be "handled" gently, that they simply not be abused by the telepathic community. The fact of their humanity does not seem to register for Mary.

Similar to Doro's long-running trials of breeding, Mary and the Patternists also conduct experiments on the non-telepathic humans in their midst. Patternist Ada uses the same language of ownership as she notes,

> The school psychologist was a kind of experiment. He was completely ignorant of the fact that the Patternists now owned him. He was being allowed to learn as much as he could on his own. Nothing was hidden from him. But, on the other hand, nothing was handed to him. He, and a few others like him scattered around the section, were being used to calculate just how much information ordinary mutes needed to come to understand their situation. (Butler, *Seed to Harvest* 413)

These experiments, conducted without the knowledge of those being tested, again reduce the non-telepaths to lab animals whose feelings or rights as human beings are not considered. Gauging how long it might take the "mutes" to realize that they have become enslaved mirrors tests one might conduct to gauge the self-awareness of lab rats. Mary experiences not only similar feelings of ownership over "her" telepathic people, but also over those non-telepaths, extending her god-like grasp beyond the borders of the Patternist community.

As it becomes clear that Mary must overthrow Doro to survive, she rejects these similarities to Doro, claiming that she is "not a vampire. I give in return for my taking." (Butler, *Seed to Harvest* 441). Focusing solely on her relationship with the Patternists, Mary sees herself as a symbiont who lives in a mutually beneficial relationship with "her people." She distinguishes herself from Doro by claiming to give something back to the telepaths from whose energy she feeds. However, her similarities to Doro remain clear even as she invokes the democratizing language of symbiosis in her effort to break free from Doro's control. This language is equally invoked by her fellow Patternists as they meet to discuss the impending battle: "'With the responsibility she's taken on for all that she's built here, she belongs to us, the people. To all of us.' 'I suspect she thinks it's the other way around, . . . but it wouldn't hurt if we went to some of the heads of houses and said it Jan's way" (Butler, *Seed to Harvest* 440). The Patternists take on a revolutionary language speaking "for the people" at the same time they recognize the falsehood of positioning Mary in this way. This is further evidenced upon their decision to echo Jan's revolutionary rhetoric, despite its misrepresentation, in order to drum up support for Mary's revolution among the heads of houses in the growing community.

The same contradictory, democratizing language is embedded in the official histories that Patternists begin to construct for themselves via "learning blocks." The inanimate objects are imbued with the history of the Pattern via psychometry as a means of inducting new Patternists into their shared, nationalist history. Other blocks serve to teach new members the "section's rules and regulations" and allow them choices as to the role they play in the new society, so long as they adhere to their appropriate place within that hierarchical system. These histories are locked in the blocks and are accessible via touch but cannot be altered by the touch of the users. This is made clear in an exchange between Mary and fellow Patternist Jan, who is able to tap into the imprints humans have left on objects with which they have interacted. Handling a fragment of a 6,500-year-old clay jar, Mary is stunned at the "purity" of the memories of the Neolithic woman who fashioned the jar. Noting that the jar had been buried largely since the Neolithic age, Jan commented that she needed only to remove the few memories of the archaeologists who had found the piece and "freeze" the story to keep herself and others from disturbing it. While the "purity" of the story comes directly from the memory of the woman who created the jar, Jan's role in curating that memory becomes clear as she describes the process of removing unwanted memories and codifying them into official histories, never to be altered again. This vision of history also recalls Nora's notion of distinction between history and memory.

Seeing the possibility for the creation of an official history of the Patternists, Mary quickly shares an idea about Jan's potential contribution to the Pattern: "A new art. A new form of education and entertainment—better than the movies, because you really live it, and you absorb it quicker and more completely than you do books" (Butler, *Seed to Harvest* 411). This quote reveals multiple functions of the learning blocks as an official history. In the same way the Patternists reclaim their autonomy from Doro's control, Jan frees the memories of the Neolithic woman from the archaeologists who would interpret her experience. The intent for both groups is one of reconstitution and preservation. Paradoxically, the act of "freezing" the moment, particularly as the Patternists reconstruct their own history after the moment has passed for use as an educational tool, constitutes the claim of universal authority that marks it as an official history. The memories of the users who might otherwise influence the "pure" history of the piece are cast off, unwanted, unsought. They can only "absorb" the history. They cannot write it. It is the putative purity of the piece that marks it as an official history rather than a *lieu de mémoire*.

As the community flourishes in numbers and power, the cost of that growth becomes clear in an exchange about the "mutes" who care for the Patternists' children between Ada, a Patternist, and a young telepathic woman, Paige, about to reach transition and take her place within Patternist society:

"They're not telepaths."

"They're slaves!" Her tone was accusing.

"Yes."

Page was silent for a moment, startled by Ada's willingness to admit such a thing. "Just like that? Yes, you make slaves of people? I'm going to be a part of a group that makes slaves of people?"

. . . "I'm not pretending that theirs is the best possible way of life, Page—although they think it is. . . . But we, our kind, couldn't exist long without them." (Butler, *Seed to Harvest* 416–17)

This brief exchange reveals that the new Patternist system requires specific forms of labor and, like Doro's race-building colonies, is unconcerned with the desires of those laboring bodies. The sole difference between Doro's system and the Patternist regime appears to be that the Patternists exercise an even greater level of social control in which the people whose labor is being demanded no longer have the agency to even feel horror at their degraded status. Their telepathic overlords force them to "enjoy" their work and see their lives of service as "the best possible way of life." The Patternists use this rationalization for enslaving non-telepaths as necessary evil as a means of comforting themselves and dismissing the young woman's critique of their oppressive regime.

This system that demands non-telepathic caretakers for Patternist children, and the creation of official histories to justify this, echoes the growth of colonial powers, which required both slave labor and accompanying rationalizing discourses. As an example of these discourses, one might turn to North American chattel slavery and the creation of the diagnosis of drapetomania, a disorder that caused slaves to flee even their kindly captors, constructed by Dr. Samuel Cartwright (Washington 36). The diagnosis allowed scientists, slave owners, and the general populace to comfort themselves with the thought that a slave's desire to be free results not from his humanity and desire for autonomy, but rather from a nervous condition for which medical science could cure. In *Mind of My Mind*, the "cure" for non-telepaths' discomfort at being forced into a life of slavery is mental control at such a deep level that the "mutes" are not even able to register their own dissent. The term "mute" takes on multiple meanings with this reading. Not only are the non-telepaths "mute" in their ability to communicate via the same means as the Patternists, but they are unable to articulate their authentic thoughts and emotions even to themselves.

By highlighting Mary's proprietary feelings and the Patternists' enslavement of non-telepaths, Butler posits that Mary's growing power within the Patternist community not only corrupts her as she seeks escape, but also encourages her fellow Patternists to make excuses for their oppressive behaviors. Aside from Page's realization of the fate of the "mutes," only Anyanwu, a seemingly immortal shape-shifter with a differing perspective on this "official" history, sees the repetition of past injustices as this new regime builds itself on the backs of a subjugated people.

Anyanwu's Resistance as *Lieu de Mémoire*

Anyanwu provides the major voice of resistance to the Patternist society in the novel. Her long life and previous relationship with Doro position her as *lieu de mémoire* which seeks to revive history in order to demonstrate the problematic recreation of Doro's colonialist structure under this "new" regime. As Pierre Nora notes, "the most fundamental purpose of the *lieu de mémoire* is to stop time, to block the work of forgetting, to establish the state of things, to immortalize death, to materialize the immaterial" (295–96). While Anyanwu cannot literally "stop time," she, as an immortal figure, does exist outside of the normal bounds of time and can, and does, attempt to obstruct the pressures to romanticize the past.

It is equally important to note that while Anyanwu retains the ability to shape-shift, she, unlike Doro, "wear[s] the same body she was born into." (Butler, *Seed to Harvest* 263). In this way, she is similar to the monument as *lieu de mémoire*. Monuments are built to stand the test of time, marking events that occurred at a particular site, deaths that occurred, or lives that were lived, reminding those that witness the monument of these events, not letting them pass into obscurity. Anyanwu performs a similar function. Throughout history, she remains, changing from time to time, but housed within her own body. Her sharp memory of the events of her life, which she shares in the form of writing, serves to remind those that read them of past events.

In addition to her exceptional recollection of all events she has experienced, the permanence of her identity within the house of her body, no matter the body's ability to shift, mark Anyanwu as a figure of stability who stands outside of time and "blocks the work of forgetting." Gregory Hampton reads Anyanwu's shape-shifting ability as evidence of the notion of the body as a text where "Anyanwu is a page already inscribed with a partial history waiting to be revised by Doro and her own experiences" (27). This claim, however, deprives Anyanwu of her agency within the novel. While she surely is changed by Doro's intervention in her life, she does not simply wait to be revised by Doro. The entire novel is the struggle of Doro's attempt to control Anyanwu and her ability, despite his manipulations, to remain in control of her identity. Further, this view of her as a text, "already inscribed with a partial history" only tells half the tale. Surely, as a Black woman, Anyanwu's body is inscribed with meaning by larger societal forces. She is not simply a tool of history, but rather a speaker for history.

Scholars of African American literature such as Melvin Dixon and Andrée-Anne Kekeh have taken the *lieu de mémoire* to represent "a tool to regain and reconstruct not just the past but history itself." (Dixon 18–19). Or a "potent repository . . . to undermine . . . paternalistic discourse"—to "tell a tale of resistance" (Kekeh 219). While Nora points to some aspects of power in the construction of history and the ways that even official histories are not the closed loops of self-reinforcing narrative, open to alteration only by sanctioned authors, he misses a critique of how race, gender, sexuality, and other categories of difference impact the construction of narrative and the authorizing of contributors to official history. What Dixon and Kekeh add to our understanding of *lieu de mémoire* is the racialized and gendered power dynamics at work in the constitution of official history and the power of the disruption of that history through *lieu de mémoire*. It is precisely this power, the possibility of cultural reform during a moment of political shift, that forms the center of my argument concerning *Mind of My Mind* and *Wild Seed*.

Kekeh's article "Sherley Anne Williams' *Dessa Rose*: History and the Disruptive Power of Memory" traces the crucial role that memory plays in the "achievement of freedom and voice" of the main character in that novel. Via her memory, Dessa Rose is able to respond to the paternalistic discourses of Mrs. Refuel, posing a threat to the entire structure of slavery. Kekeh notes the novel addresses the ways that memory and voice "make some space in official and historical discourse that has often negated them" (219). Dessa Rose's resistance to this official history is to act as a storyteller who "masters the art of controlling and telling the narrative in the course of the novel" (Kekeh 220). It is in a similar way that Anyanwu's memory functions as a means of resistance to the threat of Mary's domination and as a warning of the pitfalls that lay ahead.

While Dessa Rose ultimately achieves freedom from slavery, employing storytelling to disrupt the system that enslaves her, the specter of Anyanwu's failure to alter the course of Patternist society looms in the story. However, to read Anyanwu as a failure is to mistake where the responsibility lies in the replication of troubling power dynamics. Anyanwu clearly articulates her history not only in *Wild Seed*, but, perhaps more crucially, in *Mind of My Mind*. In the prologue, she has begun recording her memory in a trilogy of historical novels highly acclaimed by critics to be a marvel of realism. She refers to these novels as her "history," eschewing the distinction between her memory and the canonized history written from a white male perspective. In addition, she makes herself available to Mary for guidance. It is ultimately Mary's failure to consult Anyanwu as *lieu de mémoire* that allows her unquestioning belief that oppression of "mutes" is in the best interest of Patternist society. Responsibility for social change lies not solely in the hands of those who carry the memory of oppression to speak to power, but also those in positions of privilege, in this case, Mary, to recognize the value of the remembrances of Others and take heed.

As Greg Tate notes, science fiction very frequently warns readers about the "potential for catastrophe in a society when its members don't pay attention to the paths that either a new technology or an aberrant life form may take" (Dery 208). Additionally, Sandra M. Grayson argues, in her reading of gendered power in the series, that "*Wild Seed, Mind of My Mind,* and *Patternmaster* point to ancient African nations as memory and serve as reminders of pre-colonial African civilizations—times and places when women and men were equals; when women, independent of men, ruled nations and held other positions of leadership. These novels also project traditional beliefs of ancient African nations" (Grayson 40). In *Mind of My Mind* and *Wild Seed*, the tendency of science fiction to warn about the future is fused with projections of precolonial African memory that could serve to carve a path out of Doro's destructive colonial power over the telepaths that Mary's regime threatens to reconstruct. Concerning the importance of memory, Butler herself noted, "I don't think it would be wise . . . for any black person . . . to forget. Part of the strength of any people is their memory of what they've come through as a people. Part of their insurance against losing what they've gained is their memory of what their lives were like before those gains. Part of their hope for the future may be based on a knowledge of their successes in the past" (Butler, "Letter to Doubleday").

Wild Seed's narrative structure equally interrogates the play between history and historiography. As Govan notes, Butler plays with the historical novel providing a frame that corresponds to extradiegetic historical events and a space within to interpolate a speculative history (Govan, "Homage"). The reader is treated to Anyanwu's early life in Book 1—1690, reflecting Butler's thorough research of various African tribes including the Adu, the Idu, the Igbo or Onitsha people of Eastern Nigeria (Govan, "Homage" 83). Anyanwu herself is the speculative embodiment of a "legendary Igbo heroine, a magical shapeshifter and village protector" (Thaler 20). In an act of critical fabulation, Butler conjures a more fully realized character than the difficult-to-locate figure within the Western archive. Consistent with Hartman's definition, Thaler notes that "by integrating these speculative figures in the history of North American slavery, they are historical participants but do not change the past" (20).

Thaler argues that this play with history and the interpolated spaces where unfamiliar, but historically plausible, events occur "do not interrogate the representation of the past; instead the past functions as a temporal setting for a moral tale" that foregrounds a Black Atlantic perspective on Western modernity" (21). While she interprets the novel as an allegory that evokes timelessness using the Black Atlantic as a backdrop to create a universally applicable narrative, I would argue, as Hamilton does, that the Black body cannot be unmoored from time:

> Black bodies are always already mired in time. Race has a historicity to it, and connecting the idea of the somatope to the black body, particularly the black female body, does not elide time but instead brings time back into the formulation of the somatope as a body-time-space. Most importantly for my argument, the idea of the somatopic black body creates a terminology that represents the inseparability of the black body, space, and time.

Bakhtin originally tried to think of a way to articulate the inability of time and space to be separated, and in African American and Black Atlantic literatures, the black body is one of the most powerful forces holding both time and space in constant tension while operating as a dialogical site that produces meaning. (33)

Neither can we sever Butler's work from her Black identity or her repeated stated intentions of using storytelling mechanisms to instruct Black readers. In the sense of creating an instructive narrative, *Wild Seed* may be taken as allegory, but to invoke timelessness or reduce the importance of the history of Black Atlantic in the novel rejects Butler's interest in not only learning Black history, but bringing that history to her readers in a way that offers a balm to the brutal realism of *Kindred* and that extends Black history beyond the history of colonization.

Anyanwu acts as a site of memory in multiple crucial moments throughout *Mind of My Mind*. As mentioned above, Anyanwu writes a trilogy of historical novels. No longer does the work of authenticating history belong solely to those constructing "official histories." Her "history," written in the form of fiction, positions Anyanwu firmly outside of "official" histories and allows her not to just reconstruct her lived experiences, but to restructure the very way histories are told.

Anyanwu uses her personal relationships with Karl and Mary, her hand in raising each, to remind them of their humble beginnings as they become "too high" and begin to forget "where they come from." We also come to understand that she has become a companion of sorts to Doro, his sole connection to what little is left of his humanity. As a result of Anyanwu's intervention, Doro no longer kills his people once they have served his purpose. They are left to find some semblance of freedom after they have completed their child-rearing. In this way, her memory acts as a touchstone for Doro, Karl, and Mary to "block the work of forgetting" their origins, particularly as Karl and Mary begin to construct an origin myth for themselves and the Patternist society they are building that severs this history. The Patternists archive only their own origin story, perceiving their world as a new world. This origin story, which begins with the destruction of Doro, is divorced from the history of race in the larger context of the Western world and enacts an historical amnesia. Anyanwu refuses this amnesia and speaks forcefully to cast doubt on Mary's altruistic intentions, referring to her as "ruthless, egotistical, power-hungry" and "terrifying."

Doro's feelings of ownership are further evidenced as Anyanwu reflects on the meaning of Doro's request that she procreate with Isaac in *Wild Seed*: "He was not casting her aside for any reason at all. He was merely breeding her as one bred cattle and goats. He had said it: 'I want children of your body and his.' What she wanted meant nothing. Did one ask a cow or a nanny goat whether it wished to be bred?" (Butler, *Seed to Harvest* 116). Anyanwu, believing herself to be Doro's wife, and therefore in a relationship with him that would place her in a privileged position differing from that of the others he manipulates, realizes at this moment that Doro sees her as he sees all the others, an animal to be bred at his discretion. Taken together, these moments reveal that Anyanwu has long critiqued Doro's system of power. Their relationship has continually been marked with Anyanwu's resistance to his attempts to control her body. While this history may be known to the reader, Mary, who continually overlooks Anyanwu as a potential ally, remains unaware of this history of resistance. Anyanwu, as keeper of this unofficial history, has the power to transform Mary's movement. Had Mary been able to incorporate those critiques, she might have not constructed a world in which she was the god-like center, dominating those with less power than her and her fellow Patternists.

Wild Seed, the fourth novel in the Patternist series, takes the reader to the beginnings of Patternist society. In Western Africa, Doro feels the pull of strangeness and finds a small, withered African woman, Anyanwu. The reader learns that she is many centuries old with the ability to take on any shape, human or animal, that she wishes. Doro, wanting to add her ability to the race he is building, threatens to take her children and manipulates Anyanwu into coming to his settlement in the English colonies in North America. Along this journey and alongside Anyanwu, the reader is ushered through the routes of the trans-Atlantic slave trade, as Anyanwu learns more about Doro's plans for humanity. What she had originally understood as a partnership with Doro reveals itself to be a form of enslavement, and, even with all her strength, Anyanwu finds herself at Doro's mercy. After bearing him many children, she can no longer take the way he treats "his people," murdering casually, or taking them needlessly when they no longer can serve their purpose in his race-building plan. Pushed to the brink, she takes the shape of a large bird and flies away. Realizing that he cannot sense her "difference" when she takes the form of an animal, she lives for many years among dolphins. Doro, again sensing her pull, finds that she has returned to humanity and lives on a plantation with her new family, posing as her family's white male master for the benefit of outsiders. Despairing that she has been located again, Anyanwu resolves to die. Realizing that his last shred of humanity will pass away with the only other immortal he knows, Doro convinces Anyanwu to stay alive by promising to let those who he no longer sees as purposeful live out the rest of their lives in peace.

Wild Seed, whose story takes place before the events in *Mind of My Mind*, reveals earlier instances in which Anyanwu has taken up the role of the *lieu de mémoire*. Her memory extends beyond the bounds of Doro's appearance in her village. In fact, via her alternating roles as tribal historian, healer, witch, and god, she acts as cultural touchstone within her own African community (Govan, "Connections" 83). As an immortal figure, she cannot live within the confines of her community and is transformed at turns into a "witch" or a "god," occasionally to be destroyed or venerated. Located outside the bounds of humanity, she has become a memorial figure, a supernatural griot who carries the history of her community in her long memory. Anyanwu shares her cultural memory in a conservation with Doro in *Wild Seed*: "We crossed [the Niger] long ago. . . . Children born in that time have grown old and died. We were Ado and Idu, subject to Benin before the crossing. Then we fought with Benin and crossed the river to Onitsha to become free people, our own masters" (Butler, *Seed to Harvest* 10).

Anywanu is keenly aware of the need to remember the history of African and African Americans through her own experience living as a white man in *Wild Seed*. While tending to business in New Orleans, Anyanwu is passed on the street by a group of chained slaves being led to the slave pens. A latent telepath in the group, sensing her identity as an African woman, calls out to her in her mother tongue, "Anyanwu! Does that white skin cover your eyes too?" She realizes that she had been mentally running through a detailed to-do list and had not even registered the presence of slaves walking next to her. In relating the story to Doro, Anyanwu comments "I was not seeing the slaves in front of me. I would not have thought I could be oblivious to such a thing. I had been white too long. I needed someone to say what he said to me" (Butler, *Seed to Harvest* 191). In this exchange, Anyanwu reveals that in living as a white man and experiencing the privileges attached to white masculinity in the US, she had begun to adopt the colonialist framework and the ravages of slavery were beginning to become invisible to her. Indeed, Anyanwu had found herself in need of a *lieu de mémoire* to remind her of her own identity and to "block the work of forgetting" that can occur in moving to a position of privilege.

By opposing the historical amnesia of the Patternists, Anyanwu becomes a *lieu de mémoire* who acts to "establish the state of things" and "tell a tale of resistance" in her attempt to draw attention to their rising power. This resistance is felt quite powerfully in a conversation with Doro:

> "They've completely taken over the best section of town. They did it quietly, but still Mary thought it safest for them to control key mutes in city

hall, in the police department, in—" "Mutes!" He looked annoyed, probably with himself. "It's a convenient term. People without telepathic voices. Ordinary people." "I know what it means, Doro. I knew the first time I heard Mary use it. It means n*****s!" "Em—" "I tell you, you're out of control, Doro. You're not one of them. You're not a telepath. And if you don't think they look down on us non-telepaths, us n*****s, the whole rest of humanity, you're not paying attention." (Butler, *Seed to Harvest* 395)

This exchange, in which Anyanwu suggests that the Patternist's derogatory categorization of non-telepaths as "mutes" echoes language used to dehumanize African Americans throughout American history, demonstrates Anyanwu as the sole voice who recognizes the destructive potential of the community. She urges Doro to pay attention to the coming changes so that he might survive them.

Anyanwu's relationship with Doro, in part, makes Mary skeptical of her as a potential ally when Mary's own relationship with Doro began to sour. However, Butler does position Anyanwu as a potential ally throughout the novel. For instance, on the day of Mary's involuntary wedding to Karl, Mary left their shared house and returned to Anyanwu's home. There, Anyanwu advised Mary to sit and wait, so that Doro might "hear" the message she was sending. In helping Mary to register her resistance in a more effective way, Anyanwu is positioned in the story as an ally. While she may not advocate killing Doro, as the prologue to *Mind of My Mind* reveals, Anyanwu no longer supports his brutal system. However, Mary refuses to see her in this way. Surprised by Doro's request to marry Karl, Mary reveals her thoughts about Anyanwu: "Somehow, I'd never thought of myself as just another of Doro's breeders—just another Goddamn brood mare. Rina was. [Anyanwu] was for sure. But me, I was special" (Butler, *Seed to Harvest* 280). Later as Mary moves against Doro, she had long since dismissed the notion that Anyanwu might be able to contribute in some way other than being a broodmare in Doro's system. Mary had placed a telepathic marker on her, revealing her casual ownership of non-telepaths or "mutes." What these moments of dismissal of Anyanwu as an ally reveal is Mary's internalization of the colonial gaze. Under the yoke of colonialism, Anyanwu's history of furthering Doro's aims by bearing children, whether willingly complicit or not, cannot be interpreted as anything other than that of a "brood mare." By refusing to register Anyanwu's agency, Mary reveals the degree to which she has internalized colonialism's view of herself and others like her.

Where it is clear that Mary and her Pattern are at a crossroads with the potential to envision a more liberatory system, Mary's investment in the colonial gaze blocks her ability to understand Anyanwu's importance as a resource. The Patternists' position in Doro's society, both as individual telepaths before the creation of the Pattern and as joined telepaths within the mental network, are similar to anticolonial intelligentsias of the British Empire. The Patternists hold an elite position as Doro's strongest telepaths. As such, he avoids killing them by "taking" their bodies, giving them broader leeway to make decisions for themselves; however, recognizing their importance lies beyond serving as a form of sustenance for him, they remain under the yoke of Doro's colonial power and are used to further his race-building/empire-building goal.

There is untapped power in the Patternists' position. Elleke Boehmer notes the revolutionary potential of similarly placed colonized elites: "anticolonial intelligentsias, poised between the cultural traditions of home on the one hand and of their education on the other, occupied a site of potentially productive inbetweenness where they might observe other resistance histories and political approaches in order to work out how themselves to proceed" (21). The potential for liberation situated in the "inbetweenness" of the Patternists is the exact point at which the *lieu de mémoire* could be the most effective. Anyanwu has access to many other resistance histories and, in fact, has become a keeper of unofficial histories through her writing. Were Mary to recognize her importance as an ally and resource, Anyanwu could have been enormously useful in planning how to proceed. The Patternists, as anticolonial intelligentsias reaching a crossroads where a new system may be built, fail to take Anyanwu's warning into account. In doing so, they leave their own privilege unchecked and ultimately recreate the same political structure they had tried to destroy, now with a "native" figurehead in the form of Mary.

That the Patternist series tells its tale going backward through time, beginning with the end of the saga, *Patternmaster*, lends Mary's story a kind of inevitability. Mary is destined to become the first patternmaster, the pattern must survive and grow to become the feudal network of powerful telepathic overlords we see in *Patternmaster*. As such, the reader is aware that Anyanwu's intervention in this moment cannot drastically alter the course of events. While it may be tempting to suggest that Anyanwu's failure to bring about social change despite her long memory leaves little hope for our own ability to do the same, it is not Anyanwu's failure to share her understanding of the past that causes Mary to recreate these systems of power. Rather, the fault lies in a combination of Mary's failure to listen, to access the wealth of knowledge that Anyanwu provides both in her person and in her written work and the Pattern as a hierarchical system that was bound to reproduce these unexamined problematic power structures. However, her presence and resistance to the development of Patternist society in what becomes the last years of her life are important for us as we think about the dangers of building social movements that refuse to engage histories of oppression. The moment of rupture between the old and the new provides a critical opportunity for the examination of political movements. As Butler suggests, we must consult not just official histories, but sites of memory that function outside the boundaries of these histories to critique political movements as they move forward so that new regimes might actually offer the liberation that they promise. As E. Frances White reminds us, "many eloquent African writers have warned us about the problems that came from accepting a false unity during the decolonization phase that has led to the transfer of local power from an expatriate elite to an indigenous one" (85). *Wild Seed* and *Mind of My Mind* can be read alongside the work of Ngugi wa Thiongo, Sembene Ousmane, and Chinua Achebe as a similar exploration of the dangers of this false unity.

CONCLUSION

Next Steps as We Recognize the World Is on Fire

As I write this, I am again faced with the frustrations of our time: the ongoing global COVID-19 pandemic and the growing awareness of long COVID, the effects of which are just beginning to be understood; the overturning of *Roe v. Wade* and the devastating understanding that my legal rights to determine my own bodily autonomy as a person with a uterus have been distinctly curtailed; fears of a coming attack on *Obergefell*, which would threaten the ability of my friends and family to create legal familial structures; the ongoing police violence toward unarmed Black people and mass shootings that have recommenced in earnest as we emerge from our COVID-19 quarantine cocoons; the growing environmental disruptions of climate change that have produced yet another year of record high temperatures, heat waves that leave humans dead across the planet and kill thousands of livestock in fields, superstorms that dump three times the amount of rain typical for the summer period, and drought conditions in India and across the Horn of Africa, which threaten crops and leave tens of millions of people facing starvation and also create conditions for devastating flash floods as the soil dries and becomes aquaphobic; international wars that threaten wheat supplies; an oncoming global famine signaling potential future wars for natural resources like water and arable land; the growing presence of white supremacists in the US and across Europe; and the ongoing genocide of Palestinians at the hand of the Israeli government.

In the face of these conditions, I am immediately reminded of the world of Butler's *Parable of the Sower,* filled with economic, political, and environmental uncertainties that leave even the formerly upper-middle class on the edge of precarity. I imagine the citizens of *Parable of the Talents,* questioning the need for space programs when there are so many devastating problems at home on Earth. I imagine the face of a world like the one in which we live, and it would be fair to ask, What use is there in revisiting the stories of Black women and their attention to memory? So many have answered this already. Science fiction is a visionary genre and provides potential pathways forward. We have warnings of what may occur if these shadows remain unchanged. Returning to these novels now takes on an imperative to consider the lessons available in the work of these women as movement intellectuals. Beyond the future-casting and the suggested approaches to living in Lauren Oya Olamina's world that Butler offers in the Parable series, where community creation, political attentiveness, and education are key to "shaping change," Black women writing speculative fiction demonstrate how an understanding of the past and how we remember it are just as important in any project that purports to save ourselves from ourselves.

The stories of Black women writing speculative fiction trace the refusal to adopt a linear model of time in which the unrealized ambitions and approaches of earlier struggles for racial and gendered liberation are not abandoned in the name of progress. It is not forbidden to go back for what was left behind. Indeed, their "sankofarration" annotates those cultural pressures of the Western world to move forward with unquestioned official histories and pushes back with restorative fabulation and critical reversals. Considering the power of these ideas is increasingly important as the US attempts to ban critical race theory and the complicated historical narratives it brings to the fore from classrooms, in a clumsy attempt to reinstate or reinforce an overarching national narrative in the name of "constitutional originalism" and the interpretation of the framers of US Constitution as "genius auteurs" whose work and methods are beyond reproach. While these attempts are broad as they cast critical race theory as the monster of conservative nightmares, they happen in a nation where courts are packed with conservative judges and gerrymandering gives greater weight to Republican votes despite their minority in actual popular support. These attacks could very well succeed. However, this highlights the importance of popular storytelling, once again. As official avenues are foreclosed, storytelling continues to provide an underground site of gathering and sharing.

While the defeat of *Roe v. Wade* hangs heavy, as adrienne maree brown reminds us, we must take the long view of history that the iterative element of emergent strategy, and, I would argue, sankofarration provides. When we look at the history of Black folks moving toward liberation in the US, we see a pattern that looks very different from the "river of progress" that is often depicted in history texts. We note wins and losses, the gains of the Reconstruction period moving Black folks into positions of authority, gaining social and political power with the right to vote, own property, and receive an education, only to see these same advances knocked back the installation of Jim and Jane Crow policies. Frustratingly, these rights were not to be regained in some instances for almost one hundred years. Taking stock of our current setbacks, we note the gutting of the Voting Rights Act and the wave of disenfranchisement attempts made in its wake alongside the overturning of *Roe v. Wade* and the threat to *Obergefell* coming swiftly behind. Despite the devastation of these historical and recent events, we can also take comfort from the recognition of these iterations and implement a studied and intentional approach that learns from past movements to understand which actions were taken, which were successful, and which were not but which might be employed again with another outcome, as well as novel approaches our times provide us. We must create ourselves and participate in the creation of the worlds that we want to see along with the other dreamers of new worlds that we call activists. One of my favorite elements of Octavia E. Butler's writing is the simple language she uses to explore such earth-shattering and complex notions. How can we task ourselves not to just write accessibly as scholars but to write in those places where we will be heard? How can our work be used in conjunction with others to support the ongoing work to create these more just worlds?

The work of activist scholars like adrienne maree brown, Rasheedah Phillips, and Ayana Jamieson inspire me so deeply in their ability to focus our collective restorative fabulation, creating a praxis for acting in the world. These folx create workshops like Black Quantum Futurism's Time Camps that hold space for us to develop revolutionary ideas about decolonization, time, and the power of memory to heal real-world problems. They bring together artists, activists, and intellectuals to dehierarchize knowledge production in ways that allow for remarkable cross-pollination of ideas. Creating networks of these sites remembers the church basements and pews, kitchen tables, campfires, barrooms, backrooms, barber and beauty shops, bookstores, and all the other locales where relationships and community action have been born.

Grounding these lessons in practical experience is another means by which these ideas extend beyond the academy and into community spaces. Community gardens have increasingly become a powerful locus for learning, organizing, imagining, and creating new worlds. Soul Fire Farm's mission to educate and inspire is an example of this, as is the mission of Keep Growing Detroit to create a food-sovereign city. While growing food might not, on the surface, appear to have much to do with speculative fiction, it is an arm of Afrofuturist activism. Black and Indigenous agricultural practices have insight to be gleaned about temporality and the cycles of our planet as well as lessons about our relationship with the Earth. Tending the soil, serving as a caretaker or guardian of the land, is a very different approach than the desire to shape the planet to suit human desires regardless of the impact on other forms of life. In the Western world, this relationship to land and Earth has been a way of marking BIPOC as the antithesis of technology, where technology and progress are understood as a means of distancing ourselves from the patterns of the planet: providing light beyond the hours of the day the sun is visible wherever we may live, the ability to grow and procure produce beyond its seasonal availability, the attempt to seal our living and working spaces from any form of life that we do not specifically invite in. This binary opposition of technology and/or progress, marked as white and Western, and so-called primitive cultures constructed as its antithesis dismisses the observations and innovations that have historically emerged and continue to emerge outside of the Western world.

When we define technology as less of an expression of our human domination of nature and more as a means to communicate and more fully integrate ourselves into the natural world—to understand how other forms of life communicate, how we might communicate with them, what we might learn from them—broad possibilities open up for rethinking long-term existence on our planet. It reminds us that the technology we create is also a part of nature, in that it is immediately incorporated into our world through use and waste and that everything we produce is made from existing molecules, the atoms available on our planet. It also speaks back to those approaches that reject BIPOC knowledge production as anti-technological. It allows us to understand the ways that, in the US in particular, we've been systematically removed from nonurbanized locations; refused access to the waterways from which we might feed ourselves; and removed to lands that are loaded with industrial and biomedical waste or, as both inside and outside the US, have become dumping grounds for the leftover technological consumer goods that have reached their planned obsolescence. But we have also learned as Black Americans to reject those same nonurbanized locations in various cultural adaptations or a series of decrees about what Black people "don't do": swimming, hiking, farming, and roughing it are all immediately dismissed as either the pastimes of white people or a painful reminder of our own history of bondage. But the pleasure of tending the earth, the hard work and the rewards, are a part of our shared history as well. One that restorative fabulation can help us to remember and regain access to. Storytelling, the exploration of the trauma and the joy, the tropes of science fiction and fantasy to allow us to recapture our fascination with the natural world, calling attention to the ways that temporality and our understanding of the history of the world beyond the Anthropocene, how others envision their relationship to the land as one of caretaking rather than dominance, offer ways to spark the imagination, to decolonize it. At the same time, the grounding of these storytelling practices alongside gardening and farming are exactly the type of liberatory practices that unite the theoretical with the practical.

A further holistic approach, restorative fabulation provides a framework for understanding and incorporating emotion into our applications. Challenging the notion that we must always maintain an objective view in the archive, restorative fabulation refuses to reject our human emotional responses to work in ways that, according to patriarchal models, render us weak or overly feminine. In Black studies and women's and gender studies, we are called to recognize the embodied role of historical figures, authors, artists, and theorists. This requires a holistic incorporation of emotions and the physical responses they engender within us and the relationship that has to our work as artists, activists, and intellectuals. This work has already begun in the scholarship of Sami Schalk and Therí A. Pickens who unite Blackness, the body via an exploration of disability, and Black speculative fiction. Pickens's *Black Madness: Mad Blackness*, for instance, explores mental illness and Black identity through the frame of literary scholarship, where the consideration of race and ability are necessary for antiracist and anti-ableist futures. Taken alongside the previously mentioned ways that progress is marked as white, dismissing the contributions of Black folks, we must also explore mental illness when and where it intersects with flagrant expression of emotions, particularly where emotional expression has been such an important vector of oppression against Black people as "too loud" and "over-expressive" and women as "overly emotional" and thereby unable to perform logic and reason. As a site where emotions are welcome, restorative fabulation in the worlds of Black women writing speculative fiction provides a space for respite from our horrors, a place to refresh, and a place to consider our options in responding the injustices and threats to our existence as we learn about our past and imagine our potential futures.

BIBLIOGRAPHY

Anatol, Gisella Liza. "The Sea-People of Nalo Hopkinson's *The New Moon's Arms*: Reconceptualizing Paul Gilroy's The Black Atlantic through Considerations of Myth and Motherhood." *Diasporic Women's Writing of the Black Atlantic: (En)Gendering Literature and Performance*, edited by Emilia María Durán-Almarza and Esther Álvarez-López, Routledge, 2014, pp. 202–17.

Austen, Ralph A. "The Moral Economy of Witchcraft: An Essay in Comparative History." *Modernity and Its Malcontents: Ritual and Power in Postcolonial Africa*, edited by Jean Comaroff and John L. Comaroff, U of Chicago P, 1993, pp. 89–110.

Baggini, Julian. "About Time: Why Western Philosophy Can Only Teach Us So Much." *The Guardian*, 25 Sept. 2018, https://www.theguardian.com/news/2018/sep/25/about-time-why-western-philosophy-can-only-teach-us-so-much.

Barthold, Bonnie J. *Black Time: Fiction of African, the Caribbean, and the United States.* Yale UP, 1981.

Beecham, John. *Ashantee and the Gold Coast.* Dawsons of Pall Mall, 1968.

Boehmer, Elleke. *Empire, the National, and the Postcolonial 1890–1920: Resistance in Interaction.* Oxford UP, 2002.

Brooks, Kinitra D. *Searching for Sycorax: Black Women's Haunting of Contemporary Literature.* Rutgers UP, 2018.

Brooks, Kinitra D., Alexis McGee, and Stephanie Schoellman. "Speculative Sankofarration: Haunting Black Women in Contemporary Horror Fiction." *Obsidian*, vol. 42, no. 12, 2016, pp. 237–48.

brown, adrienne maree. *Emergent Strategy: Shaping Change, Shaping Worlds.* AKPress, 2017.

Brown, Jayna. *Black Utopias: Speculative Life and the Music of Other Worlds.* Duke UP, 2021.

Brown, Karen McCarthy. *Mama Lola: A Vodou Priestess in Brooklyn.* U of California P, 2001.

Burnett, Joshua Yu. "'Isn't Realist Fiction Enough?': On African Speculative Fiction." *Mosaic: A Journal for the Interdisciplinary Study of Literature,* vol. 52, no. 3, 2019, pp. 119–35.

Burton-Rose, Daniel. "The Lit Interview: Octavia Butler." *Conversations with Octavia Butler,* edited by Conseula Francis, U of Mississippi P, 2010, pp. 196–205.

Butler, Octavia E. Box 80. OEB 1513. Octavia E. Butler Papers 1933–2006. The Huntington Library, San Marino, California.

———. Box 146. OEB 2927. Octavia E. Butler Papers 1933–2006. The Huntington Library, San Marino, California.

———. Box 179. Commonplace book (large). OEB 3227. 17 Apr. 1984. Octavia E. Butler Papers 1933–2006. The Huntington Library, San Marino, California.

———. Box 327. Octavia E. Butler Papers 1933–2006. The Huntington Library, San Marino, California.

———. *Clarion Journal* 1970–1973. Box 22. OEB 298. Octavia E. Butler Papers 1933–2006. The Huntington Library, San Marino, California.

———. Letter to Doubleday and Company. 2 May 1977. Box 209. OEB 3902. Octavia E. Butler Papers 1933–2006. The Huntington Library, San Marino, California.

———. *Journal.* 10 May–16 July 1976. Box 57. OEB 1002. Octavia E. Butler Papers 1933–2006. The Huntington Library, San Marino, California.

———. *Kindred.* Beacon Press, 1979.

———. *Seed to Harvest.* Warner Books, 2007.

Camp, Stephanie M. H. "The Pleasures of Resistance: Enslaved Women and Body Politics in the Plantation South, 1830–1861." *Journal of Southern History,* vol. 68, no. 3, 2002, pp. 533–72.

Candyman. Directed by Bernard Rose, Polygram Filmed Entertainment, 1992.

Caruth, Cathy. *Trauma: Explorations in Memory.* Johns Hopkins UP, 1995.

Coded Bias. Directed by Shalini Kantayya, 7th Media Empire, 2020.

Collings Eves, Rosalyn. "A Recipe for Remembrance: Memory and Identity in African-American Cookbooks." *Rhetoric Review,* vol. 24, no. 3, 2005, pp. 280–97.

Cooper, Brittney. *Eloquent Rage: A Black Feminist Discovers Her Superpower.* St. Martin's Press, 2018.

Creary, Nicholas M. *African Intellectuals and Decolonization.* Ohio UP, 2012.

Davis, Christina. "Interview with Toni Morrison." *Toni Morrison: Critical Perspectives Past and Present,* edited by Henry Louis Gates Jr. and K. A. Appiah, Amistad, 1993, pp. 412–20.

Dery, Mark. "Black to the Future: Interviews with Samuel R. Delaney, Greg Tate, and Tricia Rose." *Flame Wars: The Discourse of Cyberculture,* edited by Mark Dery, Duke UP, 1994, pp. 179–222.

Diaz, Natalie. "Toward Alongsideness." University of Cincinnati. April 2022, Lecture.

Dixon, Melvin. "The Black Writer's Use of Memory." *History and Memory in African American Culture*, edited by Geneviève Fabre and Robert O'Meally, Oxford UP, 1994, pp. 18–27.

Donadey, Anne. "African American and Francophone Postcolonial Memory: Octavia E. Butler's *Kindred* and Assia Djebar's *La femme sans sepulture*." *Research in African Literatures*, no. 39, 2008, 65–81.

Drewal, Henry John. "Mami Wata and Santa Marta: Imag(in)ing Selves and Others in Africa and the Americas." *Images and Empires: Visuality in Colonial and Postcolonial Africa*, edited by Paul Landau and Susan Griffin, Oxford UP, 2002, pp. 193–210.

Drewal, Henry John, Charles Gore, and Michelle Kisliuk. "Siren Serenades: Music for Mami Wata and Other Water Spirits in Africa." *Music of the Sirens*, edited by Linda Austern and Inna Naroditskaya, Indiana UP, 2006, pp. 294–316.

Due, Tananarive. *The Good House*. Washington Square Press, 2004.

Edoro, Ainehi. "Aliens in Lagos: The Futuristic Lagos of Nnedi Okorafor's Sci-Fi Novel, 'Lagoon.'" *Africa Is a Country*, 31 July 2015, https://africasacountry.com/2015/07/the-futuristic-lagos-of-nnedi-okorafors-lagoon.

Eshun, Kodwo. "Further Considerations of Afrofuturism." *CR: The New Centennial Review*, vol. 3, no. 2, 2003, pp. 287–302.

Evans, Shari. "From Hierarchical Behavior to Strategic Amnesia: Structures of Memory and Forgetting in Octavia Butler's *Fledgling*." *Strange Matings: Science Fiction, Feminism, African American Voices, and Octavia E. Butler*, edited by Rebecca J. Holden and Nisi Shawl, Aqueduct Press, 2013, pp. 237–62.

Eyerman, Ron. "Cultural Trauma: Slavery and the Formation of African American Identity." *Cultural Trauma and Collective Identity*, edited by Jeffrey C. Alexander et al., U of California P, 2004, pp. 60–111.

Ezeliora, Osita. "Colonial Discourse, Poetic Language, and the Igbo Masquerading Culture in Ezenwa-Ohaeto's *The Voice of the Night Masquerade*." *Journal of African Studies*, vol. 21, no. 1, 2009, pp. 43–63.

Fabre, Geneviève, and Robert O'Meally. Introduction. *History and Memory in African American Culture*, edited by Geneviève Fabre and Robert O'Meally, Oxford UP, 1994, pp. 3–17.

Fanon, Franz. *Black Skin, White Masks*. Grove Press, 2008.

Feng, Pin-chia. "Rituals of Rememory: Afro-Caribbean Religions in *Myal* and *It Begins with Tears*." *MELUS*, vol. 27, no. 1, 2002, pp. 149–75.

Gallagher, Susan VanZanten. Introduction. *Postcolonial Literature and the Biblical Call for Justice*, UP of Mississippi, 1994, pp. 3–33.

Gaskins, Nettrice R. "Mami Wata Remixed: The Mermaid in Contemporary African-American Culture." *Scaled in Success: The Internationalisation of the Mermaid*, edited by Philip Hartman, Indiana UP, 2018, pp. 195–208.

Gill, Josie. *Biofictions: Race, Genetics, and the Contemporary Novel*. Bloomsbury Academic, 2020, https://openresearchlibrary.org/content/3aa4cb44-45b1-4656-bb45-8ac932c1275c.

Govan, Sandra Y. "Connections, Links, and Extended Networks: Patterns in Octavia E. Butler's Science Fiction." *Black Literature Forum*, no. 18, 1984, pp. 82–87.

———. "Homage to Tradition: Octavia Butler Renovates the Historical Novel." *MELUS*, vol. 13, no. 1–2, 1986, pp. 79–96.

Grayson, Sandra M. *Visions of the Third Millennium: Black Science Fiction Novelists Write the Future*. Africa World Press, 2002.

Hamilton, Regina. "The Somatopic Black Female Body in Archipelagic Space and Time in Octavia Butler's *Wild Seed*." *Human Contradictions in Octavia E. Butler's Work*, edited by Martin Japtok and Jerry Rafiki Jenkins, Palgrave MacMillan, 2020, pp. 29–49.

Hampton, Gregory Jerome. *Changing Bodies in the Fiction of Octavia E. Butler: Slaves, Aliens, and Vampires*. Lexington Books, 2010.

Harris, Lakeesha J. "Healing through (Re)Membering and (Re)Claiming Ancestral Knowledge about Black Witch Magic." *Black Women's Liberatory Pedagogies: Resistance, Transformation, and Healing within and Beyond the Academy*, edited by Olivia N. Perlow et al., Palgrave MacMillan, 2018, pp. 245–63.

Hartman, Saidiya. "Venus in Two Acts." *Small Axe: A Journal of Criticism*, vol. 12, no. 2, 2008, pp. 2–14.

Hartmann, Ivor W. Introduction. *AfroSF: Science Fiction by African Writers*, edited by Ivor W. Hartmann, StoryTime Publishing, 2012.

Hazzard-Donald, Katrina. *Mojo Workin': The Old African American Hoodoo System*. U of Illinois P, 2012.

Holloway, Karla F. C. *Moorings and Metaphors: Figures of Culture and Gender in Black Women's Literature*. Rutgers UP, 1992.

Hopkinson, Nalo. Introduction. *So Long Been Dreaming: Postcolonial Science Fiction and Fantasy*, edited by Nalo Hopkinson and Uppinder Mehan, Arsenal Pulp Press, 2004, pp. 7–9.

———. *The New Moon's Arms*. Grand Central Publishing, 2007.

Imani, Nikitah Okembe-RA. "The Implications of Africa-Centered Conceptions of Time and Space for Quantitative Theorizing: Limitations of Paradigmatically-Bound Philosophical Meta-Assumptions." *Journal of Pan African Studies*, vol. 5, no. 4, 2012, pp. 101–11.

Joseph, George. "African Literature." *Understanding Contemporary Africa*, 4th ed., edited by April A. Gordon and Donald L. Gordon, Lynne Rienner Publishers, 2007, pp. 351–96.

Jue, Melody. "Intimate Objectivity: On Nnedi Okorafor's Oceanic Afrofuturism." *WSQ: Women's Studies Quarterly*, vol. 45, no. 1–2, 2017, pp. 171–88.

Kahiu, Wanuri. "Africa and Science Fiction: Meeting with Wanuri Kahiu." https://www.youtube.com/watch?v=SWMtgD9O6PU, December 2013.

Kekeh, Andrée-Anne. "Sherley Anne Williams' *Dessa Rose*: History and the Disruptive Power of Memory." *History and Memory in African American Culture*, edited by Geneviève Fabre and Robert O'Meally, Oxford UP, 1994, pp. 219–27.

Kim, Youngmin. "Cosmogony as Political Philosophy." *Philosophy East and West*, vol. 58, no. 1, pp. 108–25.

Krishnan, Madhu. "Mami Wata and the Occluded Feminine in Anglophone Nigerian-Igbo Literature." *Research in African Literatures*, vol. 43, no. 1, 2012, pp. 1–18.

Lorde, Audre. "Uses of Anger: Women Responding to Racism." *Sister Outsider: Essays and Speeches by Audre Lorde*, Crossing, 1984, pp. 124–33.

Luckhurst, Roger. *The Trauma Question*. Routledge, 2008.

Maduka, Chidi T. "African Religious Beliefs in Literary Imagination: *Obganje* and *Abiku* in Chinua Achebe, J. P. Clark and Wole Soyinka." *Journal of Commonwealth Literature*, vol. 22, no. 1, 1987, pp. 17–30.

Martin, Kameelah L. *Conjuring Moments in African American Literature: Women, Spirit Work, and Other Such Hoodoo*. Palgrave MacMillan, 2012.

———. *Envisioning Black Feminist Voodoo Aesthetics: African Spirituality in American Cinema*. Lexington Books, 2016.

Mbembe, Achille. *On the Postcolony*. U of California P, 2001.

McGregory, Jerrilyn. "Nalo Hopkinson's Approach to Speculative Fiction." *Femspec*, vol. 6, no. 1, 2005, pp. 3–17.

McKay, Nellie Y. "The Journals of Charlotte L. Forten-Grimké: *Les Lieux de Mémoire* in African-American Women's Autobiography." *History and Memory in African American Culture*, edited by Geneviève Fabre and Robert O'Meally, Oxford UP, 1994, pp. 261–71.

Mehan, Uppinder. "Final Thoughts." *So Long Been Dreaming: Postcolonial Science Fiction and Fantasy*, edited by Nalo Hopkinson and Uppinder Mehan, Arsenal Pulp Press, 2004, pp. 269–71.

Morris, Susana M. "Black Girls Are from the Future: Afrofuturist Feminism in Octavia E. Butler's *Fledgling*." *Women's Studies Quarterly*, vol. 40, no. 3–4, 2012, pp. 146–66.

———. "Black Women and Theories of the Future." *Black Feminist Futures Series*, Schomburg Center for Research in Black Culture, 19 Feb. 2022.

———. "More Than Human: Black Feminisms of the Future in Jewelle Gomez's *The Gilda Stories*." *Black Scholar*, vol. 46, no. 2, 2016, pp. 33–45.

Morrison, Toni. *Beloved*. Vintage, 2007.

———. "Rootedness: The Ancestor as Foundation." *Toni Morrison: What Moves at the Margin*, edited by Carolyn C. Denard, UP of Mississippi, 2008, pp. 56–64.

Ndlovu-Gatsheni, Sabelo J. *Coloniality of Power in Postcolonial Africa: Myths of Decolonization*. Council for the Development of Social Science in Africa, 2013.

Ngũgĩ wa Thiong'o. *Decolonising the Mind: The Politics of Language in African Literature*. Heinemann Educational Books, 1992.

Noble, Safiya Umoja. *Algorithms of Oppression: How Search Engines Reinforce Racism*. New York UP, 2018.

Nora, Pierre. "Between Memory and History: *Les Lieux de Mémoire*." *History and Memory in African American Culture*, edited by Geneviève Fabre and Robert O'Meally, Oxford UP, 1994, pp. 284–300.

Okorafor, Nnedi. "Africanfuturism Defined." http://nnedi.blogspot.com/2019/10/africanfuturism-defined.html.

———. "Insight into *Lagoon*." http://nnedi.blogspot.com/2015/09/insight-into-lagoon.html.

———. *Lagoon*. Saga Press, 2014, Kindle AZW File.

Okorafor-Mbachu, Nnedi. "Of Course People Can Fly." *Afro-Future Females*, edited by Marleen S. Barr, The Ohio State UP, 2009, pp. 131.

Okpalaoka, Chinwe L. Ezueh. *(Im)migrations, Relations, and Identities: Negotiating Cultural Memory, Diaspora, and African (American) Identities*. Peter Lang, 2014.

Parker, Kendra. *She Bites Back: Black Female Vampires in African American Women's Novels, 1977–2011*. Lexington Books, 2019.

Patterson, Kathy Davis. "'Haunting Back': Vampire Subjectivity in The Gilda Stories." *Speculative Black Women: Magic, Fantasy, and the Supernatural*, special issue of *Femspec*, edited by Gwendolyn D. Pough and Yolanda Hood, vol. 6, no. 1, 2005, pp. 35–57.

Patton, Venetria K. *The Grasp That Reaches Beyond the Grave*. State U of New York P, 2013.

Phillips, Rasheedah, ed. *Black Quantum Futurism: Theory and Practice*. House of Future Sciences Books, 2016.

———. "Future." *Keywords for Radicals: The Contested Vocabulary of Late-Capitalist Struggle*, edited by Kelly Fritsch, Clare O'Connor, and AK Thompson, AK Press, 2016, pp. 167–74.

———. *Telescoping Effect: Part One*. Unim Press, 2017.

Prescod-Weinstein, Chanda. "Making Black Women Scientists under White Empiricism: The Racialization of Epistemology in Physics." *Signs: Journal of Women in Culture and Society*, vol. 45, no. 2, 2020, pp. 421–47.

Richard, Thelma Shinn. "Defining Kindred: Octavia Butler's Postcolonial Perspective." *Obsidian III: Literature in the African Diaspora*, 2006, pp. 118–34.

Rieder, John. *Colonialism and the Emergence of Science Fiction*. Wesleyan UP, 2008.

Rutledge, Gregory E. "Speaking in Tongues: An Interview with Science Fiction Writer Nalo Hopkinson." *African American Review*, vol. 33, no. 4, 1999, p. 589.

Schreiber, Evelyn Jaffe. *Race, Trauma, and Home in the Novels of Toni Morrison*. Louisiana State UP, 2010.

Schuman, Howard, and Jacqueline Scott. "Generations and Collective Memories." *American Sociological Review*, vol. 54, no. 3, 1989, pp. 359–81.

Setka, Stella. "Haunted by the Past: Traumatic Rememory and Black Feminism in Gayl Jones's *Corregidora*." *Mosaic: A Journal for the Interdisciplinary Study of Literature*, vol. 47, no. 1, 2014, pp. 129–44.

———. "Phantasmic Reincarnation: Igbo Cosmology in Octavia Butler's *Kindred*." *MELUS*, vol. 41, no. 1, 2016, pp. 93–124.

Sharpe, Christina. *In the Wake: On Blackness and Being*. Duke UP, 2016.

Sneed, Roger A. *The Dreamer and the Dream: Afrofuturism and Black Religious Thought*. The Ohio State UP, 2021.

Spillers, Hortense. "Mama's Baby, Papa's Maybe: An American Grammar Book." *Diacritics: A Review of Contemporary Criticism*, vol. 17, no. 2, 1987, pp. 65–81.

Streeby, Shelley. "Radical Reproduction: Octavia E. Butler's HistoFuturist Archiving as Speculative Theory." *Women's Studies: An Interdisciplinary Journal*, vol. 47, no. 7., 2018, pp. 719–32, https://www.tandfonline.com/doi/full/10.1080/00497878.2018.1518619.

Stripiaan, Alex. "The Ever-Changing Face of Watermama in Suriname: Watar Goddess in Creolization since the Seventeenth Century." *Sacred Waters: The Many Faces of Mama Wata/mami watam and Other Water Spirits in Africa and the Afro-Atlantic World*, edited by Henry John Drewal, Indiana UP, 2008, pp. 525–51.

Terry, Jennifer. "Time Lapse and Time Capsules: The Chronopolitics of Octavia E. Butler's Fiction." *Women's Studies*, vol. 48, no. 1, pp. 26–46.

Thaler, Ingrid. *Black Atlantic Speculative Fictions: Octavia E. Butler, Jewelle Gomez, and Nalo Hopkinson*. Routledge, 2010.

Thomas, Dexter. "Why Everyone's Saying 'Black Girls Are Magic'" *Los Angeles Times*, 9 Sept. 2015, https://www.latimes.com/nation/nationnow/la-na-nn-everyones-saying-black-girls-are-magic-20150909-htmlstory.html.

Tolliver, S. R. *Recovering Black Storytelling in Qualitative Research*. Routledge, 2021.

Ugwu, Ifeanyi. "Traditional Nigerian Theatre, Ideology and the National Question: Igbo Masquerade and Folktale Performances as Examples." *IKENGA: International Journal of Institute of African Studies*, vol. 15, April 2013, pp. 18–34.

Van der Kolk, Bessel A. *The Body Keeps the Score: Brain, Mind, and Body in the Healing of Trauma.* Penguin, 2015.

Wallace, Lewis. "Recall, Response, and Rememory." *Obsidian*, vol. 41, no. 1–2, 2015, pp. 129–37.

Washington, Harriet A. *Medical Apartheid: The Dark History of Medical Experimentation on Black Americans from Colonial Times to the Present.* Doubleday, 2006.

Wheeler, Elizabeth A. "Runoff: Afroaquanauts in Landscapes of Sacrifice." *Literary Afrofuturism in the Twenty-First Century*, edited by Isiah Lavender III and Lisa Yaszek, The Ohio State UP, 2020.

White, E. Frances. "Africa on My Mind: Gender, Counterdiscourse, and African American Nationalism." *Journal of Women's History*, no. 2, 1990, pp. 73–97.

"WTF Is Retrocausality?" *YouTube*, uploaded by Seeker, 8 June 2018, https://www.youtube.com/watch?v=5hYBeFNSv2o.

INDEX

activism: in academia, 1–2, 4, 12, 91; antiracist or antisexist, 4–5, 10–11, 12, 47–51, 91; gender inequities replicated within, 5–6, 12; through social media, 1–2, 66

Africa: colonialism in, legacy of and resistance to, 37–40; diaspora of, 5, 9, 14–15, 22–23, 49, 57–58, 71–73; nationalist or neocolonial forces in, 37–39, 45–46; patriarchal practices in, 47–51 (*see also* gender and sexuality); science-fiction writing in, history of, 36–38; time in (*see* time, nonlinear Afrocentric models of); traditions indigenous to, 37–50; and Western film or literature (*see* tropes, African-influenced)

African Americans. *See* Black people

African diaspora. *See* Africa

African Futurism and Afrofuturism, 5–6, 9, 12, 35–39, 55–57, 63–64, 92

African or Afrofuturist feminisms and fiction. *See* Black speculative feminisms; Black speculative fiction

American slavery: cultural and historical erasure of, 6–7, 13–14, 30; as founding trauma of African diaspora, 8, 14–16, 72–73; rationalizations for, in medicine or science, 66–67, 79; remembrance of, as tool to resist erasure and transform trauma (*see* memory work; remembrance; trauma)

ancestral time: and ancestors as family members, even after death, 14–15; as either within (Sasa) or beyond (Zamani) living memory, 11, 14–15, 54–58, 66; multigenerational horizon of, 18, 24–25; in quantum theory, 56–57; in *Telescoping Effect*, 11, 55, 66

animals: mistreatment of, or treatment of humans as, 10, 24–25, 73–76, 84; perspectives of, in fiction, 43; role of, in science fiction (*see* tropes, in genre fiction: animal-human transmutation); significance or sentience of, 30–31, 33, 43

anti-Africanness or -Blackness: at core of Western modernity, 38–39, 54; experiential harm from (*see* trauma: from colonialism or racism); human/nonhuman binaries in, 10, 38–39, 43; inequality or marginalization owing to, 13–14, 20–21, 66–67; internalization of, 20, 23–24, 37, 39–42, 49–50, 52, 62, 86; reproduced in official history, 65, 77–79; tacit in discourses of respectability, 3–4, 38–39; underlying developmental models of progress, 38–39, 50, 52–53, 57, 90–93

appropriation. *See* cultural appropriation

Bailey, Moya, 1, 4

Beecham, John, 43, 49

Beloved (Morrison), 7, 58. *See also* Morrison, Toni

Black, Indigenous, and/or People of Color (BIPOC), 11–12, 25–26, 92

Black Arts or Black Power movements, 5–6, 12, 64

Black people: oppression of, activism against, justice for, or survival from (*see* activism; justice; survival); possible futures of, imagined by and for, 1–7, 11–12, 15–16, 35–39, 55–57, 66–69, 91–93 (*see also* African Futurism and Afrofuturism); relegation of, to past, 31–32, 52–55, 92 (*see also* memory work; remembrance)

—women, academic marginalization of, 1–4, 38, 64, 89; bodily autonomy of, 4, 29–30, 61, 65, 73, 78–80, 89; cultural erasure of, and efforts to counteract it (*see* erasure; memory work; remembrance); importance of, as conduit between past and present, 14–15, 24, 30–32, 54 (*see also* communities: cultural transmission within); legal death of, as mothers under slavery, 15–16; misogyny directed toward (*see* misogynoir); pathologization of, as parents, 13–16, 20, 32; strength of, stigmatized as masculine or witchcraft, 14–15, 40–42. *See also* Black speculative feminisms; gender and sexuality

Black quantum futurism, 51, 55–58, 63–64, 91

Black speculative feminisms: as Afrocentric world-building, 3, 35–51, 58–60, 67–68, 70–77, 81–88; community-orientation of, 11, 19–22, 32, 38, 46–48, 54, 61 (*see also* communities: of artists, activists, and scholars); compared with other feminisms, 3–5, 91;

ecofeminist variations on, 3–6, 12, 30–31, 37–38, 43; importance of self-definition to, 10, 55–56; vs. utopianism, 5–6, 7–9, 36–37, 69–70

Black speculative fiction: ancestral past woven with present in, 18, 55–63; bodily or experiential knowledge in, 3–4, 12, 53, 83; as both exposing and modeling recovery from racist violence, 6, 8–9; counter-narratives within, 6–7, 14–15, 20, 59–60; empathy and emotion in, as transformative, 4, 8, 27–28, 34, 40, 54, 61–63, 93; as healing tool for trauma, 3–4, 6–10, 17, 20–26, 32, 49, 53–54, 91; as memory work (*see* memory work); multiple genres of, hybridity in, 3–4, 26–27 (*see also* horror genre; science fiction); paradigm shifts anticipated in and catalyzed through, 3–4, 49–51, 52, 82–83; as social-justice tool, 2, 5–6, 60, 90–93; temporalities of, as nonlinear and non-Western, 52–53; as tool for cultural memory and historical recovery, 8, 14, 53–54; as visionary, 3, 6, 10, 35, 50, 90. *See also* restorative fabulations

—African, 35, 57, 63–64. *See also Lagoon*

—Caribbean, 10, 16, 20–21. *See also New Moon's Arms, The*

—North American, 2, 9, 16–18, 37, 57. *See also Kindred*; Patternist series; *Telescoping Effect*

—other authors of. *See* Bailey, Moya; Brooks, Kinitra; Gumbs, Alexis Pauline; Hairston, Andrea; Ireland, Justina; Imarisha, Walidah; Jamieson, Ayana; Jemison, N. K.; Johnson, Alaya; brown, adrienne maree; Martin, Kameelah L.; Morris, Susana M.; Pickens, Therí; Schalk, Sami; Shawl, Nisi; Solomon, Rivers

Black Womyn Time Camp, 51–52

bodily autonomy. *See under* gender and sexuality

Brooks, Kinitra, 3–4, 17–18

brown, adrienne maree, 4–6, 9, 12, 35, 90–91

Brown, Karen McCarthy, 18–19

Butler, Octavia E.: annotations and archive of, 2–3, 6, 58–60; memory work of, 2–4, 8–11, 54; restorative

INDEX • 105

fabulations of, 7–11, 59–63, 82 (*see also* restorative fabulations); as speculative fiction writer, 7, 9, 12, 54, 58–63, 67–68; on time or time travel, 57, 59–60. See also *Kindred*; Parable series; Patternist series
Butler Legacy Network, 4–5

Candyman (dir. Rose, 1992), 13, 20
chronopolitics, 4–5, 5n3, 55–60, 67–68
cognitive estrangement, 5–6, 50, 62
Collins, Patricia Hill, 14, 66–67
colonialism, 6, 10–11, 35–50, 53–68, 78–87. *See also* decolonization
communities: alienation from, 6, 17–21, 24–27, 34, 46–47, 61, 76, 89; of artists, activists, and scholars, 12, 35–36, 56, 64, 69, 91; bonds to or within, 13, 17, 20, 31–32, 47–52, 54, 73–88; ceremonial or common spaces of, 11, 16, 20–21, 47, 90–92; cultural transmission within, 3, 20–27, 35–36, 53–54, 64–66 (*see also* memory work; remembrance); emphasis on, in Africa (*see* tropes, African-influenced: communalism); healing of or within, 6, 9, 17, 20–24, 32; importance of elders in, 19–20, 27, 31, 64–66; nonmembers of, treatment of, 43–44; norms or stigmas within, 12, 34, 45–52; power structures in, 73–88; threats to or violence against, 9, 15–19, 33–34, 40
—outsider communities: power structures replicated in, 70–79; restorative models of, 79–88; of slaves or other fugitives, 30–31, 33–34, 73–86
Cooper, Brittney, 3–4
counter-narratives, 14–15, 19, 58–60
Creary, Nicholas M., 38–39
critical fabulations: neo-slave narratives as (*see* neo-slave narratives); as painful but necessary memory work (*see* memory work); reconstructions of traumatic history in, 6–7, 82–83; vs. restorative fabulations (*see* restorative fabulations)
critical race theory, 13, 90
cultural appropriation: of African or Black traditions, 13–14, 20–21, 40–41, 64 (*see also* tropes, African-influenced); of Black women's knowledge production, 57–58, 64–66

decolonization: of both race and gender, 47–51; of imagination, 5–7, 55–56, 93; of inner life and self-perception, 2, 12; of knowledge production, 91; of postcolonial nations, 87–88; of Western temporality (*see* Telescoping Effect)
disruption: of dominant culture, 1–2, 55–56, 81, 89
Due, Tananarive. See *Good House, The*
dystopias. *See* utopianism

ecofeminism, 3–6, 12, 30–31, 37–38
emotions and empathy, 7–11, 27–34, 49–50, 59–64, 72–74, 79, 93
environmental justice, 3–6, 12, 30–31, 37–38
epigenetics, 58–65. *See also* families; history; memory
erasure: in attacks on critical race studies, 13, 90; of Black presence in imagined futures (*see* futures: erasure of Black presence in); of living memory by official history, 70–72, 79; of reality of oppression, 16–18, 29–31, 80; resistance against (*see* memory work; remembrance); as symbolic violence, 33–34, 36
Eshun, Kodwo, 5n3, 12, 55, 58–59, 67. *See also* chronopolitics
Eurocentrism, 8, 38, 49, 53–56, 67
exclusion: within academia, 1–2, 4, 91; within activist or independence movements, 6, 12, 38–39; from communities (*see* communities); from white social order (*see* Jim / Jane Crow policies)

families: ancestors as members of (*see* ancestral time); genetic entanglements of, 61; histories of, 9–11, 14–15, 20, 22, 26–27, 33, 63–65; mother-daughter relationships in, 14–15, 32
Fanon, Franz, 38, 55
feminisms. *See* Black speculative feminisms

folklore tradition, 14, 16–18, 21, 30, 33, 47, 70–71
food justice, 5–6, 92
forgetting. *See* erasure; remembrance
futures: as Black and feminist, 1, 12; erasure of Black presence in, 1–5, 11; fiction's role in casting and creating, 2, 12, 35–37; gleaned from memory or history, 2, 60; self-direction and shaping of, 12, 60; Western or white monopolization of, 55. *See also* survival
futurism. *See* African Futurism and Afrofuturism

gender and sexuality: activism relating to (*see* activism: antiracist or antisexist); in Africa, history of equity in, 81–82; animus or inequity based on, 6, 10–11, 28, 34, 39–42, 47–48, 65–67; of Black mothers, masculinity and hypersexuality ascribed to, 14–15, 32; bodily autonomy in, 4, 29–30, 61, 65, 72–73, 78–79, 89; domestic violence based on, 37, 41, 61, 89; and internalized homophobia or sexism, 10–12, 23–24, 28–29, 73, 78–79; marginalization of, in official history, 15, 80–81; nonnormative, 23–24, 28–29, 32–33, 75, 80; renewed threats against liberation of, 73–74, 90
Good House, The (Due), 2, 9–10, 13–26, 27, 33; tropes repurposed in (*see* tropes, in genre fiction: Vodou)
Govan, Sandra Y., 82, 85
Grayson, Sandra M., 81–82
Gumbs, Alexis Pauline, 4–5

Hairston, Andrea, 9
Hamilton, Virginia, 16, 27, 82–83
Hartman, Saidiya, 4, 6–8, 82
haunting. *See under* tropes, in genre fiction
historical realism, 3, 7–11, 58–59, 61–63, 83
history: cycles and repetitions in, 11, 69–70, 71–79; diasporic or familial (*see* Africa: diaspora of; families: histories of); official, as static and filtered vs. lived experience, 70–72, 79; recovery of, when suppressed or marginalized, 6–7, 11, 55–56; shifts in present worldview from reconstructions of, 6–7, 82–83. *See also* erasure; memory work; remembrance
Holloway, Karla F. C., 15, 58
Hopkinson, Nalo. *See New Moon's Arms, The*
horror genre: family secrets in, 9–10, 35–51; folkloric traditions and, 17; memory in, as traumatic vs. celebratory, 16–17; racism in, as itself an object of terror, 3, 9, 17–18; survival in, as communal vs. individual, 20, 21–24, 25–26; tropes repurposed in (*see* tropes, in genre fiction: haunting; possession; telepathy); white American conventions of, 13, 17–18. *See also Good House, The*; *New Moon's Arms, The*

imagination: decolonization of, 5–6, 55–56; of inclusive and just futures, 11–12, 15–16, 35–39, 55–57, 66–69, 91–93; as meaning-making or worldbuilding, 1–12, 20, 27–28, 50–59, 63, 90–93; mobilized for social justice (*see* Black speculative fiction: as social-justice tool); poverty of, in racist discourses, 8–9; vs. romance or utopianism, 5–6, 7–9, 36–37, 69–70
Imani, Nikitah Okembe-RA, 56–57
Imarisha, Walidah, 9, 35
Indigenous peoples, 5, 11–12, 19–20, 24–26, 37–38, 92
Ireland, Justina, 9

Jamieson, Ayana, 4, 91
Jemison, N. K., 9
Jennings, John, 11, 56. *See also* sankofarration (term)
Jim / Jane Crow policies, 26, 53, 91
Johnson, Alaya, 9
justice: generational, 24–25; precarity of progress in, 89–90. *See also* environmental justice; restorative justice

Kahiu, Wanuri, 36
Kekeh, Andree-Anne, 80–81
Kindred (Butler): ancestral or familial connections in, 58–59, 61–63;

characters in, humanized despite dehumanizing conditions, 7, 53; as multigenre hybrid of science fiction and historical realism, 7–11, 52–63, 83; nonlinear and recursive temporality of, 52–54, 57–61; as restorative fabulation, 7–8; role of witnessing in, 8, 54, 62–63; tropes repurposed in (*see* tropes, in genre fiction: time travel)

Lagoon (Okorafor), 2, 10, 35–45, 48–50; tropes repurposed in (*see* tropes, in genre fiction: alien invasion as colonization)
LGBTQ+ or queer people, 6, 28–29, 34, 44
lieux de mémoire (memory spaces), 11–12, 69–72, 74–81, 85, 87. *See also* Patternist series
Lorde, Audre, 3–4
Luckhurst, Roger, 52–53

magical realism, 3–4, 15, 26–27
Martin, Kameelah L., 4, 14, 21, 23
masquerade, 45–47
Mbembe, Achille, 39, 42
Mbiti, John, 11, 54
memory: collective or cultural, 3–4, 11, 13–34, 65, 80; as dynamic mode vs. history, 70–71; familial, 9–11, 14–15, 20, 22, 26–27, 33, 63–65; of horror as healing, 9–10, 20–26; importance of, for present or future, 8–9, 16; repression of, 16, 18, 27–29, 33; touchstones for (see *lieux de mémoire*). *See also* history; memory work; time
memory work: as consciousness raising (*see* wake work); as counter-history, 14–15, 19, 58–60; as cultural transmission, 3, 20–27, 35–36, 53–54, 64–66; as knowledge production, 2–4, 15–16, 38, 60, 66, 91–92; as rememory or remembrance (*see* remembrance; rememory); trauma studies as subset of, 16
Mind of My Mind (Butler). *See* Patternist series
misogynoir (term), 1–2, 40–41
Morris, Susana M., 4–5, 16
Morrison, Toni, 3, 15–16, 58

neo-slave narratives, 3, 7–11, 58–59, 63, 83. *See also Beloved*; *Kindred*
New Moon's Arms, The (Hopkinson), 2, 9–10, 17, 20–21, 26–34; tropes repurposed in (*see* tropes, in genre fiction: haunting)
Ngugi Wa Thiong'o, 38, 88
Nora, Pierre, 70–72, 76–77, 79–80

Obergefell v. Hodges, 89
OEB Legacy Network. *See* Butler Legacy Network
Okorafor, Nnedi. *See Lagoon*

Parable series (Butler): *Parable of the Sower* and *Parable of the Talents*, 4, 90
passing, racial or gendered, 80–81, 87
Patternist series (Butler): African precolonial history in, 82; as allegory of postcolonialism, 87–88; colonization of bodies, feelings, and minds in, 77–79; compulsory reproduction and eugenics depicted in, 72–73, 75–77; as critical and/or restorative fabulation, 4, 11; future- and social-world building of, 11, 69–76, 77, 81–88; history and lived or collective memory in, mediation of, 4, 11, 70–72, 74–88; protagonist of, as cultural-memory touchstone (see *lieux de mémoire*); repressive powers in, overturned then replicated, 69–70, 71–79; reverse chronology of novels in, 69n1, 70n2; tropes repurposed in (*see* tropes, in genre fiction: animal-human transmutation; possession); women's solidarity in, 86–87
—*Clay's Ark* and *Survivor*, 69–70, 69n1
—*Mind of My Mind*, 4, 11, 69–75, 69n1, 70n2, 81–88
—*Patternmaster*, 69, 69n1, 72–74, 81–82, 87
—*Wild Seed*, 4, 8, 11, 63, 69–82, 69n1, 70n2, 85–88
Patton, Venetria K., 15, 17–20
Phillips, Rasheedah: activism of, 52, 63–64; on linear time, 52, 63–64; novella and short stories of (see *Telescoping Effect*)
Pickens, Therí, 4, 93

108 • INDEX

quantum mechanics, 56–57. *See also* Black quantum futurism; retrocausality
queer or LGBTQ+ people, 6, 28–29, 34, 44

racism. *See* anti-Africanness or -Blackness
religion, 4, 18, 23–26, 29, 37–42, 47–50
remembrance: via archives of lived experience, 1–3, 6, 58–60; as critical historical reconstruction, 6–7, 82–83; vs. cultural amnesia, 20–21, 58, 71–72, 83, 85–86; as cultural or historical recovery, 6–7, 11; as resistance against erasure and not revisiting of trauma, 9–10, 13–14, 15–26, 66–67. *See also* erasure; history; memory work
rememory: in *Beloved*, 16, 27; as both transformative and traumatic, 16, 20–21, 26–27; in *The Good House*, 17–18, 20–21; in *The New Moon's Arms*, 27–28, 32–33; as presencing of past in present, 3–4, 27; as therapeutic, 3–4, 16, 20–21, 26–28
restorative fabulations: communal bonds in, 9–10; damaging tropes repurposed in, 6–9, 15, 49, 64 (*see also* tropes, in genre fiction); future- and change-orientations of, 6–7, 82; imagination as tool for world-building in, 1–12, 20, 27–28, 50–59, 63, 90–93; vs. purely critical fabulations, 6–8; vs. utopian fiction, 5–6, 7–9, 36–37, 69–70
restorative justice vs. punitive justice, 6–7
retrocausality, 57–58
Rieder, John, 35, 36, 57
Roe v. Wade, 89

sankofarration (term), 11, 54–58, 90–91
Sasa. *See* ancestral time
Schalk, Sami, 4, 93
science fiction: arts and sciences interconnected in, 67–68; cautionary tales in, 80–82, 87–88; decolonized futures in, 35–45, 48–50; decolonized time in, 63–69; escapism vs. realism of, 35, 61; as imaginative and visionary, 3, 35–39, 50–51, 90; ties of, to colonialism, 36, 57–58, 87–88; tropes in (*see* tropes, in genre fiction). *See also Kindred*; *Lagoon*; Patternist series; *Telescoping Effect*
scientific racism, 66–67, 79
Setka, Stella, 17, 58
sexuality. *See* gender and sexuality
Sharpe, Christina, 2, 52–53, 60
Shawl, Nisi, 9
slave narratives. *See* neo-slave narratives
social-justice activism. *See* activism; justice
social norms. *See* communities: norms or stigmas within
Solomon, Rivers, 9
speculative fiction. *See* Black speculative fiction
Spillers, Hortense, 13–15
storytelling, 5, 7–8, 15–16, 20, 36, 43, 62, 71, 81–83, 90–93
Streeby, Shelley, 2–3, 58–60
survival: of Black people from slavery, 20–27, 61–63, 69–70, 75–77; from cultural imperialism or racism, 5–6, 16–17, 39; of family and culture, 20–27, 62, 86–87; from linear time, 52–53; from trauma, 20–27, 29–30, 61

Telescoping Effect (Phillips): author's activism, 52–53; on Black Grandmother Paradox, 57–58, 65–66; decolonization of Western temporality in, 10–11, 54–58, 66; extra- and intertextuality of, 64; as speculative fiction, 2, 5, 9–11; title, significance of, 66; tropes repurposed in (*see* tropes, in genre fiction: cross-generational contact)
Terry, Jennifer, 59–61
Thiong'o, Ngugi wa. *See* Ngugi Wa Thiong'o
time: decolonization of, 54–57 (*see also* ancestral time; Black quantum futurism; chronopolitics; sankofarration); in developmental model of progress, 38–39, 50, 52–53, 57, 90–93; linear Western construct of, 52–53, 54–55, 66, 90; nonlinear Afrocentric models of, 56, 66–68; of oppression as iterative and recursive, 11, 53, 58 (*see also* retrocausality); of work vs. personal

life, 66. *See also* history; memory; memory work

Tolliver, Educator S. R., 8

trauma: ancestral or multigenerational, 9–10, 19–25, 29, 53–54; causality and temporality of, 52–53, 61–62; from chattel slavery (*see* American slavery); from colonialism or racism, 3–4, 5–6, 10, 14–15, 38–39, 50–51; from lost cultural or familial origins, 14–15, 18–20, 22–27; memorialized on bodies, 3, 4, 29–30, 61–62, 82–83; memory or rememory of, as therapeutic, 3–4, 9–10, 16, 20–28; reading or writing about (*see* Black speculative fiction: as healing tool for trauma); studies of, 16, 29, 54. *See also* erasure

tropes, African-influenced: ancestral presence, 14–15, 17–20, 25, 45–46, 53–63; communalism, 11, 21–22, 38, 46–47; conjurers, priestesses, or witch figures, 14, 20–21, 32, 40–41; the crossroads, 19, 44, 46–47, 86; honoring animals or sacred lands, 10, 12, 18–27, 36, 43, 91–93; nonlinear temporalities, 18, 52–57, 60, 66–68, 90; religiosity or spiritualism, 23–26; trickster figures, 44, 58, 72. *See also* cultural appropriation

tropes, in genre fiction: alien invasion as colonization, 10, 12, 35–45, 48–50 (see also *Lagoon*); animal-human transmutation, 30–31, 33–34, 36, 43, 84; cross-generational contact, 53–54, 63–66 (see also *Telescoping Effect*); haunting, 9, 13–19, 58 (see also *New Moon's Arms, The*); possession, 9–10, 15, 17–23, 41–42, 71–73 (see also Patternist series); telepathy, 42–43, 69–79, 82–88; time travel, 10–11, 52–68 (see also *Kindred*); Vodou (a.k.a. Voodoo), 9, 13–14, 18, 21 (see also *Good House, The*)

Ugwu, 46–48

utopianism, 5–6, 7–9, 36–37, 69–70

Vodou (Voodoo). *See under* tropes, African-influenced

voting rights, 90–91

wake work or woke politics, 2, 5, 21, 35–37, 42–45, 48, 53, 91. *See also* memory work

Washington, Booker T., 38–39

Wheeler, Elizabeth A., 5–6

Wild Seed (Butler). *See under* Patternist series

writing: accessibility and adaptability of, 2, 91; as collective memory or communal space, 8, 11–12, 20–21, 71, 81, 90–91 (*see also* communities: ceremonial or common spaces of); fluidity in modes of, 3–4, 10, 71; as knowing vs. understanding, 62; as meaning- or sense-making of history and identity, 2–3, 8, 23, 83; therapeutic value of (*see* Black speculative fiction: as healing tool for trauma). *See also* storytelling

Zamani. *See* ancestral time

NEW SUNS: RACE, GENDER, AND SEXUALITY IN THE SPECULATIVE
Susana M. Morris and Kinitra D. Brooks, Series Editors

Scholarly examinations of speculative fiction have been a burgeoning academic field for more than twenty-five years, but there has been a distinct lack of attention to how attending to nonhegemonic positionalities transforms our understanding of the speculative. New Suns: Race, Gender, and Sexuality in the Speculative addresses this oversight and promotes scholarship at the intersections of race, gender, sexuality, and the speculative, engaging interdisciplinary fields of research across literary, film, and cultural studies that examine multiple pasts, presents, and futures. Of particular interest are studies that offer new avenues into thinking about popular genre fictions and fan communities, including but not limited to the study of Afrofuturism, comics, ethnogothicism, ethnosurrealism, fantasy, film, futurity studies, gaming, horror, literature, science fiction, and visual studies. New Suns particularly encourages submissions that are written in a clear, accessible style that will be read both by scholars in the field as well as by nonspecialists.

Black Speculative Feminisms: Memory and Liberated Futures in Black Women's Fiction
    CASSANDRA L. JONES

Anti-Blackness and Human Monstrosity in Black American Horror Fiction
    JERRY RAFIKI JENKINS

Gendered Defenders: Marvel's Heroines in Transmedia Spaces
    EDITED BY BRYAN J. CARR AND META G. CARSTARPHEN

The Dreamer and the Dream: Afrofuturism and Black Religious Thought
    ROGER A. SNEED

Diverse Futures: Science Fiction and Authors of Color
    JOY SANCHEZ-TAYLOR

Impossible Stories: On the Space and Time of Black Destructive Creation
    JOHN MURILLO III

Literary Afrofuturism in the Twenty-First Century
    EDITED BY ISIAH LAVENDER III AND LISA YASZEK

Jordan Peele's Get Out: *Political Horror*
    EDITED BY DAWN KEETLEY

Unstable Masks: Whiteness and American Superhero Comics
    EDITED BY SEAN GUYNES AND MARTIN LUND

Afrofuturism Rising: The Literary Prehistory of a Movement
    ISIAH LAVENDER III

The Paradox of Blackness in African American Vampire Fiction
    JERRY RAFIKI JENKINS

www.ingramcontent.com/pod-product-compliance
Lightning Source LLC
Chambersburg PA
CBHW020950230426
43666CB00005B/254